Divorce:
What an Education

What You Don't Know

PATRICK VESSEY

The opinions expressed in this manuscript are solely the opinions of the author and do not represent the opinions or thoughts of the publisher. The author has represented and warranted full ownership and/or legal right to publish all the materials in this book.

Divorce: What an Education
What you don't know
All Rights Reserved.
Copyright © 2015 Patrick Vessey
v1.0

Cover Photo © 2015 thinkstockphotos.com. All rights reserved - used with permission.

This book may not be reproduced, transmitted, or stored in whole or in part by any means, including graphic, electronic, or mechanical without the express written consent of the publisher except in the case of brief quotations embodied in critical articles and reviews.

The Concept of Judgement Press

ISBN: 978-0-578-16408-3

PRINTED IN THE UNITED STATES OF AMERICA

This book is dedicated to the men and women, but mostly men, who have been mishandled, mistreated, and charged with wrongdoing within the Judicial System of Family Law and Divorce.

TABLE OF CONTENTS

1. INTRODUCTION 1
2. HISTORY OF DIVORCE 3
3. ZELDA 15
4. LAWYERS 25
5. CHILD SUPPORT 36
6. SINGLE PARENTS 48
7. CHILDREN 59
8. THE LION DOG 71
9. MATERIALISTIC WORLD 83
10. FORWARD 91
11. FATHERS' RIGHTS 98
12. SYNOPSIS 105
CREDITS 110
BIBLIOGRAPHY 112

Chapter 1
INTRODUCTION

Over the years, I've tried to find the words to express one man's journey dealing with the judicial system of family law and divorce; a journey that will leave you with the response: "this is wrong." However, you're not allowed to write about the living without their permission and my acquaintances would forbid it.

In society, there are services, agencies, and institutions that are so inundated that they can only see what's on the surface and are unwilling to look harder and deeper at the circumstances surrounding the situation to uncover the truth.

There are thousands and thousands of stories, horror stories, regarding divorce, mostly effecting men but there's a small percentage that have had an impact on women too. Usually, most women that get divorced want nothing from their partner; they just want him to go away. Sometimes, that's not the case.

I met a woman, got married to rid the family of the biological father, and adopted her children because he was detrimental to them. After I signed the court documentation and finalized the adoption, I was no longer a part of the family unit thirty days

DIVORCE: WHAT AN EDUCATION

from the exact date. This woman received sole legal and physical custody of the children, her ten-year custody battle with him had ended, and I have to take care of her for the rest of my life. I've had three attorneys, all of whom were paid by my mother over a six year period and I haven't gotten any further than when I started.

Chapter 2
HISTORY OF DIVORCE

The definition of divorce in its simplest form means to terminate a marriage contract between two people. Throughout history, statistics reveal that divorce rates have steadily increased.

The history of divorce in America dates back to the seventeenth century; the first divorce in the new world was recorded in 1639 by the Puritans in Massachusetts. Mrs. James Luxford found out her husband was married to another woman; she was awarded all of the couple's property on the grounds of bigamy. Then her husband was fined and exiled to England.

The first record of a legal divorce in the American colonies was recorded in 1643; Anne Clarke of the Massachusetts Bay Colony was granted a divorce from her absent and adulterous husband, Denis Clarke, by the Quarter Court of Boston, Massachusetts. In a signed and sealed affidavit presented to John Winthrop Jr., the son of the colony's founder, Denis Clarke admitted to abandoning his wife, with whom he had two children, for another woman with whom he had another two children. He also stated his refusal to return to his original wife, thus giving the Puritan court no option but to punish Clarke and grant a divorce to his wife, Anne. The Quarter Court's final decision read: "Anne Clarke being deserted by Denis Clarke, her husband, and his refusing to accompany with her, she is granted to be divorced." Records throughout the colonial years during the seventeenth and eighteenth centuries reveal scandals and divorces prompted by interracial adultery and fornication. In the 1770s, Thomas Paine — a political pamphleteer and editor of the Philadelphia magazine who was separated from his English wife — argued vehemently and outspokenly for divorce reform. Divorces soon became more common and somewhat less stigmatized. Desertion was one of the most common offenses cited in petitions during American colonial years according to Kenneth Jost and Marilyn Robinson in the article "What can be done to help children of divorce?"

Early feminists from the 1880s, like Elizabeth Cady Staton, crusaded for the right for divorce. "By 1880, one in sixteen U.S. marriages were ending in divorce, already the highest rate in the world" according to Charles S. Clark in the article, "Is it time to crack down on easy divorces?" the tenth of May 1996. Concerns about divorce led the anti-divorce group, the New England Divorce Reform, to conduct a study about the number of divorces. The report released in 1889 confirmed that "divorce had risen dramatically in the United States; from 9037 in 1867 to 25,535 in 1886 — more than a 150 percent increase," according to Jost and Robinson.

From 1880 to 1920, the rise in American affluence paralleled a skyrocketing divorce rate. Scholars have documented a number of economic crucial events during this time, such as the increase in standardized industrialization, increased wages, shorter work weeks and an abundance of products that enhanced homes and enriched private lives.

During the 1880s, American men were clearly the breadwinners in most households and if a man did not provide for his family financially, his wife had a good enough reason to divorce him. By the early 1900s, according to Elaine Tyler May in the Journal of Social History article, "The Pressure to Provide: Class, Consumerism, and Divorce in Urban America, 1880 - 1920"; the reasons for divorce became a little more ambiguous. The increase in consumerism and materialism led many women married to blue collar workers to get divorces because their husbands couldn't support them in the manner that is 'expected' in American society. Ironically, it seems like nothing has changed.

In the roaring 1920s when women won the right to vote and began entering the workforce, they started to openly acknowledge their sexual desires. Gilbert Hamilton, a researcher, asserted that as many as a quarter of Americans had committed adultery. In 1927, John Watson, a psychologist, predicted that marriage would end within a half century. By 1940, the divorce rate in the U.S. was two per one thousand but then, the divorce rate leveled off and actually declined a little during the 1950s; however, it began to increase again in the 1960s (Jost and Robinson.)

With the sexual revolution and women's movement in the 1960s, attitudes toward divorce began to change. Although there was still a lot of stigma about divorce in America, social policies became more liberal. The state of California led the way toward enacting the "No Fault" divorce in 1969, and soon other states quickly followed.

If you look into no fault divorce history, you would be amazed at the ease with which this controversial law was passed. It was

DIVORCE: WHAT AN EDUCATION

during the Vietnam War that the no fault divorce law took its shape. In 1969, Governor Ronald Reagan of California made what he later admitted was one of the biggest mistakes of his political life. He was seeking to eliminate the strife and deception often associated with the legal regime of fault-based divorce. Reagan signed the nation's first no fault divorce bill; the new law eliminated the need for couples to fabricate spousal wrongdoing in pursuit of divorce. Indeed, one likely reason for Reagan's decision to sign the bill was that his first wife, Jane Wyman, had unfairly accused him of "mental cruelty" to obtain a divorce in 1948. The no fault divorce also gutted marriage of its legal power to bind husband and wife; allowing one spouse to dissolve a marriage for any reason or for no reason at all. He did away entirely with the no fault system and in its place was a single action for divorce based on irreconcilable differences. Unlike in fault divorce where allegations or wrongdoing had to be proven, assertions of irreconcilable differences could be asserted by just one spouse and assumed to be true. The allegation itself is sufficient grounds for divorce. Other states that have adopted the no fault system refer to "incompatibility" or "irremediable breakdown of marriage," both of which are synonymous with California's irreconcilable differences. In a decade and a half that followed, virtually every state in the Union followed California's lead and enacted the no fault divorce Law.

Soon after 1973, the Episcopal Church changed its policy so that a marriage no longer had to be annulled before the church would allow a parishioner to remarry. The history of Christian doctrine on divorce is quite interesting; like it or not, divorce is a reality in today's society. People of Christian religious faiths get divorced just as those with no declared religious faith.

HISTORY OF DIVORCE

In Matthew 19:1-10, Jesus acknowledged that Moses had said that a man could divorce a wife; then, he went on to say that it was because of "the hardness of your hearts" that this policy was adopted. The familiar phrase from a Christian wedding, what "God hath joined together, let not man put asunder," comes from this passage.

In early days of the Christian Church, divorce was permitted on the grounds of adultery and only the "innocent" party could start a divorce action; however, even after the divorce was granted, both partners were directed to remain celibate as long as their former spouses were alive. According to the history of Christian doctrine on divorce, even if divorce were an option under civil law of the time, it was still forbidden under canon Law.

The Roman Catholic Church hasn't changed its view of marriage over the centuries; marriage is a sacrament and even if a person gets a divorce, they are still considered to be married by the Church. A Roman Catholic who's divorced is barred from remarrying while his or her spouse is still living. A Roman Catholic may apply to have his or her marriage annulled; when a marriage is annulled, it's considered not to have been a valid marriage from the beginning. The marriage can be annulled if:

- Either party didn't understand the vows or was forced to enter into the marriage
- Either party lied while taking the marriage vows

The marriage wasn't consummated if a couple's wedding is annulled, they are free to marry in the church.

The Anglican Church, also known as the "Church of England," was established by Henry VIII. Henry was a Roman Catholic who wanted to divorce his first wife, Catherine of Aragon, because she couldn't produce a male heir. He attempted to get a special dispensation so that he could divorce Catherine and marry Anne Boleyn. The dispensation wasn't granted and Henry demanded that the Archbishop of Canterbury grant him the divorce he so desperately wanted. The Archbishop granted the king his divorce and he married Anne Boleyn. Anne gave birth to a daughter, who became Queen Elizabeth 1 in due course. Henry was made supreme head of the church by a law passed in 1534. Henry's marriage to Anne Boleyn didn't last; Anne Boleyn was found guilty of treason and executed on the 19 of May 1536. Henry's fourth marriage, to Anne of Cleves, was annulled a few months after the wedding. Anne was given an annual income from Henry and had the use of a number of royal homes during her lifetime. For Anglican churches, the attitude toward divorce isn't so cut and dried. Divorced persons can remarry in the church with the permission of the local bishop. The Church understands that despite a couple's efforts to keep their marriage together; marriages do break down. In an effort to offer support and help to separated and divorced members of the congregation, a number of parishes offer support groups to those who have been recently divorced. The Christian doctrine on divorce official policy supports the view that marriage should be for life, but certain denominations have tried to deal with the fact that divorce is not an uncommon occurrence in modern times. The Roman Catholic view of divorce has remained constant throughout the ages as mentioned. The Catholic Church was still against divorce, but it did little to lobby in state capitals to change the new divorce laws.

In the 1970s, the divorce rate, which had been slowly climbing in the late 1960s, increased by almost forty percent from 1970

HISTORY OF DIVORCE

to 1975. The divorce rate in the United States continues to climb, but at a slower rate, from the 1980s, to the remainder of the decade. While divorce rates leveled off in the 1980s, experts believe they will hold steady in the future and statistics show that half of all marriages in America will end in divorce (Jost and Robinson).

The earlier Anglo American Society considered the marriage vows to be extremely valuable and important enough to last a lifetime, which was in the early years of the twentieth century. However, I feel that individuals don't believe in marriage vows anymore. Soon, it was realized that if a person is wrongfully treated by his/her spouse then he/she may be allowed to end the marriage or break the marriage vows. The law has softened a little. Now, divorce can be obtained on the "faults" basis: - Desertion or Absence - Cruelty (Physical/Emotional) – Adultery. By the 1950s, authorities realized that what was termed "cruelty" soon became the discretion of the courts. If the judges found that a particular treatment of the spouse could be defined as "cruelty", then the divorce could be granted.

Divorce laws were being continually modified and changed; soon, it was felt that there were many couples who were unhappy with the state of their marriage but more so, because the divorce laws were insufficient to meet their circumstances. Hence, by the end of the 1960s, the "grounds for divorce" was said to be modified. Then, adoption of no fault grounds from divorce was adopted as the major divorce law which allowed the spouses to divorce without providing to the court that the other spouse had committed any of the major wrongdoings that have been listed above. This law was formally adopted in 1969 as stated.

There were final touch ups given by the beginning of the 1980s which finally gave shape to the no fault divorce laws and

DIVORCE: WHAT AN EDUCATION

from then on the history of divorce has completely changed. One might consider the early grounds of divorce where the bad behavior of a spouse was coaxing enough to go for divorce, desertion or long absence are also grounds for "no fault." But, here again, the blame of the fault or reason of the break in a marriage was being attributed to one spouse. Thus, this was not no fault divorce. The law pertaining to no fault divorce simply states that there is a "breakdown of marriage" due to "incompatibility" or "difference of opinion." There's no intention to put the blame on any of the spouses but what is important is that there must be a specific period of separation (for two years, five, etc.) as declared by the law of that state, which indicates that the spouses don't have a workable marriage at all! In a nutshell, no fault divorce laws were the result of a history of divorce which literally forced couples to be together when all the while they were wishing to be separate. With these laws, divorce was a quick solution to be rid of a tragic marriage relationship that neither of the spouses wanted, though there was no hard evidence of adultery, desertion, etc.

Like marriage, divorce in the United Stated is the province of the state governments, not the Federal Government. Divorce or "dissolution of marriage" is a legal process in which a judge or other authority dissolves the bonds of matrimony existing between two persons, thus restoring them to the status of being single and permitting them to marry other individuals. The legal process for divorce may also involve issues of spousal support, child custody, child support, distribution of property and division of debt; though these matters are usually only ancillary or inconsequential to the dissolution of marriage. Divorce laws vary from state to state.

In some jurisdictions, divorce requires a party to claim fault of their partner that leads to the breakdown of marriage, but even in jurisdictions which have adopted the "no fault" principle in divorce proceedings, a court may still take into account the behavior of the parties when dividing property, debts, evaluating custody, and support.

No fault divorce on grounds such as "irreconcilable differences" or a period of living apart is now available in all states and in some states, they require a legal and/or physical separation of up to two years prior to a formal divorce decree. This legal requirement, along with couples who live in a state of separation simply because neither has sought or completed a divorce for other reasons, has led to the creation of a separate, somewhat ambiguously perceived, category of relationships - "separated."

Prior to the 1970s, divorcing spouses in many states had to allege that the other spouse was guilty of a crime or sin like abandonment or adultery; when spouses simply could not get along, spouses and their lawyers were usually able to negotiate "uncontested" divorces. The no fault divorce revolution began in Oklahoma in 1953; New York is currently the last state to allow nonconsensual no fault divorce in 2010. Every state's law provides for child support where children are involved and alimony. The median length of a marriage in the U.S. today is eleven years with 90 percent of all divorces being settled out of court.

In most jurisdictions, divorce must be certified by a court of Law to become effective. The terms of the divorce are usually determined by the court though they may take into account prenuptial agreements or postnuptial agreements or simply ratify terms that the spouses may have agreed to privately. In the absence of agreement, a contested divorce may be stressful to the spouses and lead to expensive litigation; less adversarial approaches to divorce settlement have recently emerged such as mediation and collaborative divorce which negotiate mutually acceptable resolutions to conflicts.

In cases involving children, governments have a pressing interest in ensuring that disputes between parents do not spill over into the family courts. All states now require parents to file a parenting plan when they legally separate or divorce.

Since the 1980s, Federal legislation has been enacted affecting the rights and responsibilities of divorcing spouses. For example, Federal Welfare Reform mandated the creation of child support guidelines in all fifty states during this time. Erisa includes provisions for the division of qualified retirement accounts between divorcing spouses. The Internal Revenue Service (IRS) established rules on the deductibility of alimony and Federal bankruptcy laws prohibit discharging in bankruptcy of alimony and child support obligations.

COBRA allows a divorced spouse to obtain and maintain health insurance. The laws of the state(s) of residence at the time of divorce govern divorce, not those of the location where the couple was married. All states recognize divorces granted by any other state and all states impose a minimum time of residence: Nevada currently being the briefest at six weeks.

Typically, a county court's family division hears requests for dissolution of marriages. The National Association of Women Lawyers were instrumental in convincing the American Bar Association to help create a family law section in many state courts and pushed strongly for no fault divorce law around 1960 (CF. Uniform Divorce Bill).

In some states, fault grounds remain but all states now provide other grounds as well, such as various terms: irreconcilable

HISTORY OF DIVORCE

differences, irremediable breakdown, loss of affection or similar. For such grounds, no fault need be proven and little defense is possible. However, most states require mutual consent and/or a waiting period from six months to two years of separation. Some have argued that the lack of means to contest a no fault divorce makes a marriage contract the easiest of all contracts to dissolve. In recent years, some have begun to favor moderate divorce reforms such as requiring mutual consent for no fault divorce but no such laws have been passed as of this writing.

Fault grounds, when available, are sometimes still sought, which may be enacted where it reduces the waiting period otherwise required or possibly in hopes of affecting decisions related to divorce such as child custody, child support, alimony and so on. States vary and can be contested with respect to child-related matters and finances.

Mediation is an alternative way of resolving divorce issues. Similar in concept collaborative law is where both sides are represented by attorneys but commit to negotiating a settlement without engaging in litigation. States vary in their rules for division of assets in divorce. Some states are "Community Property" states but most are "Equitable Distribution" states and others have elements of both. Most community property states start with the presumption that community assets will be divided equally, whereas, equitable distribution states presume fairness may dictate more or less than half of the assets will be awarded to one spouse or the other. An attempt is made to assure the welfare of any minor children generally through their dependency. Thus, the spouse given custody (or spouse with the greater share of residence time in the case of joint custody) may receive assets to compensate their greater child care expenses. Commonly, assets acquired before the marriage are considered individual and assets acquired after are marital.

Alimony, also known as "maintenance or spousal support," is still being granted in many cases, especially in longer term marriages. Alimony is more likely in cases where a spouse has remedial needs that must be met in order for the spouse to become fully employable; for example, one spouse gave up a career opportunity or development in order to devote themselves to the family. Permanent alimony becomes likelier in lengthy marriages.

Chapter 3
ZELDA

The *Dobie Gillis Show*, originally the *Many Loves of Dobie Gillis*, was a television show that ran from 1959 to 1963. The series and some episode scripts were adapted from a 1951 collection of short stories of the same name written by Max Shulman. It inspired the 1953 film *The Affairs of Dobie Gillis* with Debbie Reynolds, Bob Fosse, and Bobby Van as Dobie Gillis.

Until the *Many Loves of Dobie Gillis* came along in September 1959, there were no TV shows centered around the lives of teenagers. Dobie Gillis holds the distinction of being the first television show to treat teens as anything other than complete dolts and probably the last to do so until "Square Pegs" in 1982.

The series revolved around a teenage Dobie Gillis (Dwayne Hickman) who aspired to have popularity, money, and the attention of beautiful and unattainable girls. He didn't have any of these qualities in abundance and the tiny crisis surrounding Dobie's lack of success made the story in each weekly episode. His partner in crime was American television's first beatnik: Maynard G. Krebs (Bob Denver).

DIVORCE: WHAT AN EDUCATION

Krebs had a deep aversion to work and was convinced life was for enjoyment. Dobie's father, Herbert T. Gillis (Frank Faylen), who owned a grocery store was only happy when Dobie was behind a broom. Dobie's father was often caught up in various elaborate get-rich-quick schemes or situational bailout a la Ralph Kramden. With Dobie getting ensnared along with him; in the end, they both came around grudgingly to Maynard's point of view.

As a high school student, Dobie lived at home with his parents in the Show's early years and his interactions with his parents was a source of much of the humor. His mother, Winnie (Florida Friebus), was very caring and perhaps tended to baby her son a little too much; his father, Herbert, was a very proud, hardworking former child of the Great Depression and a veteran of World War II. He was often heard to declare, "I've gotta kill that boy, I've just gotta!" but deep down he was a good and decent man.

Dobie's two main antagonists were rich kids, Milton Armitage (Warren Beatty) and after his departure, Milton's cousin, Chatsworth Osborne, Jr (Steven Franken). Both represented the wealth and popularity to which Dobie aspired. They both shared the same actress, Doris Packer, as their mother.

Dobie was hopelessly attracted to the money-hungry blonde Thalia Menninger (Tuesday Weld), who frequently entangled Dobie in her money-making schemes. Weld soon left the series but was replaced by a seemingly endless stream of young women equally hard for Dobie to obtain. Most, however, were not as money-obsessed as Thalia. Thalia's catch phrase was that the money wasn't for her but for her family; she would talk about ailments her family had that only money could cure. Thalia claimed her looks were all her family had to lift them out of their bad situation in life.

ZELDA

Zelda Gilroy, (Sheila James Kuehl) was a brilliant and eager young girl who was hopelessly in love with Dobie, much to his annoyance. Despite, his protests, Dobie was clearly fond of Zelda and would be married to her in the proposed 1977 series pilot, *Whatever Happened to Dobie Gillis?* Zelda claimed Dobie loved her too but just hadn't realized it yet. To prove this, she'd wiggle her nose (like a rabbit) at Dobie who would do the same back to her. However, Dobie said it was only a reflex and not love that made him do that.

The name Zelda Gilroy is embedded in the memory of anyone who has ever seen *The Many Loves of Dobie Gillis*. Zelda was the quintessential nerd; if her nose wasn't buried in a book, it was busy crinkling up in that incredibly cute way, driving Dobie daffy in the process.

Sheila James Kuehl gave the part of Zelda her nerdy all. It was a showcase role, one that afforded her a chance to display her comic gifts and earn enough money to buy a Malibu beach house and a red Porsche. But eventually, she felt that her television image eroded her identity. "I thought of myself as unattractive," says Kuehl "because that's what everyone said about Zelda."

It took a decade for the petite actress to believe in her own good looks. By then, she had given up show business and was thinking about a law career just as one can imagine Zelda herself might have.

At the time of this article the 2nd of December 1985 she was a law professor at the Los Angeles Loyola Marymount University. Kuehl devoted much of her time to women's right and exploding the kinds of sexual stereotypes that once hindered her happiness.

As a teenager, Kuehl says she "bought" Hollywood's idea that women were either comely but dumb or homely but bright.

DIVORCE: WHAT AN EDUCATION

"Some actresses back then were getting a bad rap in exactly the opposite way I was." For example, Kuehl feels that Tuesday Weld, who played Thalia Menninger, "wasn't taken seriously but she was very talented, funny, and bright," remembers Kuehl. "One time she asked me if I thought she could go to college, as if she didn't know how bright she was." That was never Kuehl's problem.

She was the daughter of a Catholic airplane construction worker and his Jewish wife. Sheila grew up in Los Angeles and glided through high school. A natural ham, she landed her first paid acting role at age eight on a radio series. "I learned about professional behavior, showing up on time, knowing my lines, not stepping on someone else's laughs," she says. Next came a six year stint on one of television's first sitcoms: *The Stu Erwin Show*. As a sophomore theater major at UCLA, Kuehl (whose stage name was Sheila James) auditioned for the role of Zelda Gilroy. "The writer, Max Shulman, said he hired me because I was the only girl who read for the role who was shorter than he was," says the 5'2" Kuehl.

On the set Kuehl's co-stars were impressed by her intelligence. "When we first met," says Bob Denver, who played Dobie's beatnik friend, Maynard G. Krebs, "I saw her breezing through a script just flipping through the pages, and I said, "You're not memorizing it that fast are you?" Embarrassed, Kuehl answered, "Yes, but please don't tell anybody."

In 1963, after four years on the air, Dobie Gillis was abruptly cancelled. Kuehl was slated for her own spinoff, *Zelda*, and four episodes were filmed but the project was dropped when rumors began to circulate that she was a lesbian. A network executive took her aside and told her that "some of the powers that be at CBS decided that she was just a little too butch." Kuehl didn't have a boyfriend in real life, but did have a girlfriend; she was expelled from a UCLA sorority when some of her sisters discovered letters to her from her lesbian lover. Like many gay and lesbian actors before her who were fearful that revelation of their sexual orientation would ruin their careers, Kuehl adopted the ruse of having a heterosexual partner, inventing a boyfriend who she could evoke in conversations on the set. However, she fell in love with a woman who was out and she began the difficult process of coming out herself. First, to her sister and later to her parents all of whom proved supportive.

She graduated from UCLA that same year and realized that she was out of school and a job at the same time. Kuehl sat in her Malibu beach house which eventually she was forced to sell and waited for the phone to ring. It never did. "I didn't leave the business," she explains, "the business left me, I couldn't get hired anymore."

She returned to UCLA first as a student adviser to campus activist groups and later as an associate dean of students. After a man in her office with less experience was promoted above her (unfairly, she felt), Kuehl became fixated on the notion that women in the workplace were treated differently from men. So, she went back to school and earned a law degree from Harvard Law School. Then she became an advocate for the rights as an attorney specializing in feminist causes such as women's rights and a tireless advocate for victims of domestic violence.

While in her third year at Harvard, she was elected class marshall and president of the law school student council, but the honor that made her proudest was winning best oralist (the first woman ever to do so) in the Ames Moot Court competition. Students simulated an argument before the U.S. Supreme Court visiting Supreme Court Justice Thurgood Marshall Strode who clasped her hand in his two huge hands and said, "Lady, I like your style."

She became a co-founder of and managing attorney for the California Women's Law Center and was elected to the California State Assembly in 1994.

Sheila Kuehl, a California State Senator from Santa Monica, Representing the seat formerly held by Tom Hayden, she was an especially virulent hater of heterosexual men. The leader in writing the nastiest of all laws in the nation on child support, alimony for life, gender based custody, domestic violence and anything else she could use as a weapon. Her hatred for men was evident in her legislative agenda and several of her colleagues in Sacramento, California had remarked on it.

When she went to Sacramento, she kicked off this first campaign with a high profile press conference manufacturing the myth that tons of women get beat up on Super Bowl Sunday by fans of the winning team. When Peter Wilson was governor, most of her bills were promptly vetoed, so she made extra nice with Gray Davis as soon as she announced the theory that a man with so few evident principles would be a perfect foil for her toxic agenda. Sure enough, Gray Davis never vetoed any one of her bills and followed her advice on vetoing those she didn't like. For example, he vetoed Rod Wright's Bill letting men falsely identified as the fathers of children off the child support hook. She was upset with Gray Davis' humiliating defeat to Arnold Schwarzenegger; she felt Arnie was going to send her back to the veto pound.

Shelia James wrote an article: "A Child Support Enforcement System that Works - What a Concept!" - May 1999. She wrote that over the past several years, it had become more and more evident that California's Child Support Enforcement System was not working for more than three million children who rely on it to make sure they get the food, shelter, clothing and medical attention they needed. The system was enforced by district attorney's offices in 58 counties, affected more California children than any state program other than public school; yet, five out of six children relying on the state's assistance were not receiving any support at all. In fact, California's child support programs were performing below the national average in most measurements of successful programs.

According to her, at the time, failures of California's child support enforcement programs were rendered even more dramatic because of living in an era of time limited welfare. When time runs out, child support payments were going to be only real "safety net" children can expect and California's net was full of holes.

Her major priority was to completely overhaul the Child Support Services System; Her legislation AB 196, specifically required the governor to appoint an undersecretary for a new Child Support Services Agency by the first of January 2000 to oversee and manage the program by the first of July in the same year, to adopt uniform standards, forms and procedures, regulations implementing nationwide "best practices" for the establishment, enforcement and collection of child support. Also, the best management practices for such programs. Counties must adopt and implement these procedures and practices by the first of September, as well as meet minimum performance standards set by the undersecretary.

The bill relieved the district attorney and required every county to set up a Department of Child Support Services reporting to the State Department of Child Support Services. This department would be established by the first of January 2001 and report to the Secretary of Health and Human Services.

Her legislation allocated the collection of all past due support to the Franchise Tax Board; allowing the district attorneys to voluntarily turn over collection of past due support to the Franchise Tax Board. They had established a successful track record. To make sure that the new county department didn't fail, the bill required new state departments to send in a team of experts to any county that requested assistance as a kind of "strike force" when counties were not meeting their minimum performance standards.

She addressed the fact that people who are working for salary and who owe child support could have their wages attached, but people working as independent contractors could not. It put the children of independent contractors on equal footing, so as a final measure, AB 196 required employers of independent contractors, by the first of July 2000, to begin regular reporting of earning information to the Employment Development Department so that these earners could be found and required to pay up what they owed. She believed these measures would improve the collection of child support in California because the kids deserved no less.

Sheila Kuehl completed two four-year terms in the California State Senate, winning the seat in 2000 and 2004. After serving for six years in the state assembly where she was the first openly gay or lesbian person to be elected to the California Legislature 2009; she was a vigorous advocate for the GLBTQ (Gay, Lesbian, Bisexual, Transgender and Queer Culture.)

Kuehl doesn't regret the fact that her screen career was short-lived. She stated, "To some extent I feel that I failed as an actress, but I don't think of it as a loss. I think of it as a doorway that opened."

ZELDA

Sheila Kuehl's days as being a California state senator and state assemblywoman have past after she termed out of both in 2008. Throughout 2009, she was a member of the California integrated waste management board. In 2010, she began a new project; Kuehl Consulting and was pleased to be asked to serve as the founding director of Public Policy Institute at Santa Monica College. Also, producer and host of eight legacy television shows detailing the history of the city of West Hollywood and co-author of "Safe at School." A policy white paper addressing how to keep schools safe for LGBT (Lesbian, Gay, Bisexual and Transgender) youths, which was produced for the Williams Institute at UCLA Law School.

In 2010 and 2011, she and former assembly member Patty Berg co-facilitated a new institute for elected women: California, bringing together over fifty women, senators and assembly members, to conduct trainings for women newly elected to the state legislature. In 2011, they began to offer the model to a number of other states. Also in 2011, she continued her tenure as director of Public Policy Institute at Santa Monica College where they established the only AA in public policy awarded at a California community college where they established six new community programs on current issues in public policy. She continued as the host of "Get Used to it," a national cable show originating in West Hollywood on LGBT (Lesbian, Gay, Bisexual and Transgender) issues and people. She began work with Planned Parenthood of California helping to develop legislation expanding access to early non-surgical abortions in California. She's working with the Williams Institute at the UCLA Law School helping to draft model state code on marriage, civil unions, and domestic partnerships.

DIVORCE: WHAT AN EDUCATION

In 2012, she had the honor to serve as a regents' professor at the School of Public Affairs, graduate school of public policy at UCLA. Her class, "Making Policy through Legislation and Rules," met for ten weeks and provided a continuing forum for the graduate and undergraduate students enrolled to consider and discuss more than thirty areas of public policy.

I sent an email to Sheila Kuehl's website and explained my situation to her briefly because she was instrumental in getting the child support revised; however, she stated, "Not sure how to respond, and usually don't when folks send me the details of their cases/families. However, if you think there might be some necessary legislation, all the legislators, including the new ones, will be looking for new bills come November. You might try Senator Ellen Corbett, as I think she understands a bit about family law."

It's ironic, the leader and voice for women had no comment, but I understand her position and wasn't about to push the issue.

Chapter 4
LAWYERS

I've succumbed to the joke about them that was used during the 1993 movie, "Philadelphia"; an American drama and one of the first mainstream Hollywood films to acknowledge HIV/AIDS.

What's five thousand lawyers at the bottom of the ocean? The answer: a good start.

The first attorney I hired was through a mutual friend; however, this man practiced family law outside the Sacramento area in Martinez, California. I should have stayed within Sacramento County where I got married and where my ex-wife filed for divorce.

As I stated earlier, I met a woman, got married to rid the family of the biological father, and adopted her children because he was detrimental to them. After I signed the court documentation and finalized the adoption, thirty days from the exact date, I was no longer a part of the family unit. As I waited for the attorney's response, I should have listened to the verbal clues during our conversation since I was new to divorce proceedings. He stated,

DIVORCE: WHAT AN EDUCATION

"Men usually don't win in court because the court is biased toward women." However, he was willing to take the case. His plan was to annul the adoption and prove to the court that this woman was a fraud. Unfortunately, I learned that you only have a year and a half to annul an adoption and the time had already passed when this was brought to my attention. Also, it's very difficult to prove fraud in a court of law.

Our first court appearance was scheduled for the 3rd of September 2003; however, I was unable to attend because my father had been accepted into the NIH-Funded Program Project for the study of Fronto temporal Dementia (FTD)/Progressive Aphasia. It's a rare form of dementia that's aggressive and can be misdiagnosed as Alzheimer's. Aphasia is the loss of a previously held ability to speak or understand spoken or written language due to disease or injury to the brain. So, he would be admitted to the University of California in San Francisco for an extensive battery of tests for three nights. My attorney was fined $1000 for appearing in court without his client (which I had to pay). If I was aware of that, I would have made an effort to return to California and appear in court. At the time, I was in Florida assisting my mother in her care for my ailing father. However, I wasn't notified of being penalized until after the fact and I don't know if my attorney explained the situation concerning my father either. So, you must be present at all of your court appointments.

We went to court on the twenty third of September 2003; the Judge proposed a payment of $2500 a month for child and spousal support. I informed my attorney that I don't make that kind of money; I don't even come close to that amount in a month. He responded, "Just sign it and pay what you can before we go to trial," so I did. Looking back, this was the first mistake that I made,

LAWYERS

because I shouldn't have signed any court documentation about which I wasn't in agreement. However, I adhered to his advice and paid my ex-wife what I could afford. Honestly, I should have tried to bypass the entire legal system because like most men, they don't take the time to educate themselves on divorce laws and custody issues according to "NO BS Divorce Strategies for Men." This is an informational guide for guys who are facing divorce and legal issues, which I highly recommend.

I received a copy of a letter from my ex-wife's attorney stating that he and his secretary had left several messages on my attorney's phone. He was requesting a return call; as of the date, October 31, 2003, her attorney hadn't received any messages whatsoever nor any word from the office of my lawyer. According to her legal counsel in a previous message he stated, "I advised that your client, Mr. Vessey, had not been paying any of his court-ordered child or spousal support. Further, that he has paid none of the attorney fees ordered. Please contact my office immediately regarding this matter to prevent further court intervention. Should another hearing be necessary because of Mr. Vessey's non-compliance of the court order, I will request all attorney fees and costs associated with such hearing as well as sanctions against Mr. Vessey." So, I called my legal counsel in regard to this correspondence and I was told to ignore it until we went to trial. However, it's a fact that less than two percent of custody disputes ever make it to trial (NO BS Divorce Strategies for Men). Basically, her attorney was proposing jail time which wasn't the first time or the last that I would be threatened with being placed there.

My legal representative was becoming concerned that I wasn't making any payments towards the court order. One of the biggest mistakes men make is letting their lawyer run the show. Lawyers are in business to make money for themselves, not help you reach a fair settlement or get custody of your kids. (NO BS Strategies Divorce for Men). I was told that I needed to make my best effort to pay at least the spousal support portion of the order. He had been doing research on setting aside the adoption and hoped to have a petition ready for filing within the next couple of weeks. He mentioned that it wasn't as simple as he originally anticipated, but if we did it just right, we could prevail on the nullification of the adoption. He stressed again the importance of making an effort to pay the support so that I wasn't in contempt (which I was). I wouldn't hear from my attorney for weeks at a time, even months. Every time I called his office, I spoke to his secretary who would constantly quote the rules and regulations of family law; I rarely spoke to my lawyer. Over the next several months, I expressed my anger and frustration toward my ex-wife along with some profanity during my phone conversations or faxed letters. Because of the recent letters, his secretary would run interference. I was quoted, "You're not paying a fourth of what the court ordered; it's in writing meaning, the child and spousal support." I just wanted to go to trial and rid myself of this woman and didn't care about committing fraud which was difficult to do in court; however, he still didn't petition the court for a trial date. I agreed to pay my ex-wife $1200 a month which I actually couldn't afford; so, my attorney requested that I send him a check and he would forward it to her. I don't think he ever did. At the beginning of 2004, I sent him $1000 so he could type and submit to the court our intentions. Once again, I hadn't heard from him in regard to settling this legal matter. So, I called his office, early May 2004, and spoke to his second assistant who informed me that he had quit the case. I explained to her that though I followed his directions I had been placed in contempt of court. His assistant got upset because she felt I was blaming the office for my legal problems, but that's not the truth. We got into an argument and she hung up the phone. My lawyer sent a letter confirming that he had resigned from this matter along with the documentation to annul the adoption. His correspondence stated and I quote, "Mr. Vessey has failed to ever take my advice since the support hearing in this matter. Mr. Vessey feels that I have failed to do my job because this court issued a child and spousal order. All communication has broken down and our relationship was non-existent. Mr. Vessey has continually written letters both to myself and paralegal which contain statements than can easily be interpreted as threats. I cannot represent a client who continually fails to follow my advice and further blames me and my staff for all of his misfortune resulting from his dissolution of marriage. Mr. Vessey refused to follow any of this court's orders and refuses to understand when I give him advice and/or attempt to explain to him that I am not personally responsible for the fact that he had been ordered to pay child and spousal support, but rather that is the law. I have tried to explain the court procedure to Mr. Vessey; however, Mr. Vessey continues to not take my advice and continues to request that I somehow "Get this over with" and "Get rid of his support obligation." Of greater concern is the threats Mr. Vessey has communicated to me, both in written correspondence and his verbal messages left with my staff when I am out of the office."

I was left in contempt of court and without an attorney because I listened to him initially when we first went to court. He didn't have the courtesy or decency to personally call and inform me of his actions; it was discovered through his second assistant, as I said. Then, he had the gall to request payment for services that he performed, which he did not.

I decided to handle the case myself which you should never do in the court of family law. My lawyer resigned and compromised my position; I spent numerous hours and days working on the computer preparing legal documentation and writing letters to submit to the court, but no success. I flew to California from Florida three times that year, spent less than twenty minutes in front of the judge and accomplished nothing.

While trying to handle my legal problems myself, I made a formal complaint against my former attorney to the California State Bar Association. I informed them that my attorney failed to provide complete representation to a client, failed to act with reasonable diligence and promptness in representing a client, communication with a client was not maintained, legal matters were incompetently handled, and paid legal fees were paid for substandard work. I included a timeline of events that transpired between him and myself. I received a letter from Cydney Batchelor, deputy trial counsel, in regards to the complaint. It stated that my attorney asked to be enrolled in the State Bar's Court Confidential Program for attorneys for substance abuse or mental health issues. It is likely that he would be accepted. As a condition precedent to my lawyer being enrolled in the program, he must admit misconduct to the extent it exists, including misconduct in my case that he handled. That has not yet happened, but as I say, I expect that it will within the next couple of weeks. As I said, the court's program is confidential and I am precluded from disclosing anymore to you about the case at this time." I called Cydney about this and I was advised that my attorney had to complete the program which was thirty-six months. Once he finished the program, I would be able to obtain the outcome.

At the end of 2004, I decided to apply for sole legal and physical custody of the children; a scare tactic. I wanted to see what type of reaction I would get from my ex-wife. I filled out the documentation, then went to the mediation date in December. I was told by the clerk at the courthouse in California, I could hand my documentation to the mediator. When my ex-wife and I entered her office, I tried to present my paperwork to Lynne Zahnely. I stated, "I was told that I could hand this to you." She replied, "Just put it in the mail." Once again, I told her that the clerk said I could hand this to you and her reply, "Just put it in the mail." I was standing in front of this woman, so I told her, "Do you realize that I'm flying back and forth from Florida" but once again, she replied, "Just put in it in the mail." I didn't get anything accomplished because this woman was biased toward my ex-wife and it was a waste of my time. As you can see, there were many obstacles and it was the last time I saw the children.

Upon my return to California, I hired a second attorney but did some research first. I had been advised to hire an attorney who attended the "McGregor School of Law." It was a highly accredited school for lawyers And, I was also told to hire an individual that was in the Sacramento area because that's where the case resided. So I enlisted the services of a female attorney and met with her in March 2005. I explained my situation to her as I did with my first legal representative about how I met a woman, got married, and adopted her children to rid the family of the biological father because he was detrimental to them. I was then released from the family unit thirty days from the exact date the court documentation was signed and the adoption finalized. I expressed to her that I wanted to annul the adoption and prove to the court that my ex-wife was a fraud. She replied, "it might be hard to prove fraud," but she was willing to take the case. I questioned her about child support and her reply was, "Don't worry about that, because they will catch up to you sooner or later."

We used the petition to set aside the adoption based on fraud that my first attorney had prepared which I received from him and submitted to the court. I did most of the work completing all of the documentation so my female attorney just had to sign her name. However, she wasn't any better than the first because she failed for the same reasons representing a client— reasons which I have explained. During the month of August 2005, I was informed that my ex-wife had been calling her office because she wanted to settle this legal matter; my ex-wife wouldn't all of a sudden want to settle unless there was some personal gain for herself. I expressed to my legal representative what I wanted to gain from the settlement; however, I didn't hear from her for two months. I wanted to know what our course of action would be before heading to this settlement conference which was scheduled for the eleventh of October. My ex-wife's lawyer prepared her petition statement and issues, contentions and proposed disposition. However, I didn't see this documentation until the day we went to court. After reviewing the documentation, I told my attorney that I didn't agree with any of it and I wanted to go to trial but every issue that I addressed with her, she would dispute it. She'd quote what the court would do. So I told her that I wanted my name removed from every joint account we had together during the marriage.

Unfortunately, I was made to sign this agreement; the second mistake I made. I shouldn't have signed it. My attorney felt that she'd made the best deal that she could at the settlement conference; she felt that I wouldn't have won at the trial and this was her firm belief. We would never have known because she didn't want to pursue that; on the contrary, she didn't make the best deal possible because I was left in the dark until the day of the conference. I probably should have reported her to the California State Bar Association as well.

I was recovering from hip replacement surgery (2006) and I needed to be present in court; however, I was unable to do so. My attorney stated that the judgment for divorce could be entered into record without my presence. I learned that my ex-wife and her attorney, along with mine, were in court to enter the judgment, so I was thinking to myself *how does this look when you proceed with the ruling without my presence, especially in the eyes of the court?*

I tried to appeal the judgment from the settlement conference through the court of appeals in the later part of 2006 and 2007. I was attempting to get the appeal documentation correct and the appropriate fees covered before it was dismissed. I received a letter on the fifth of February 2007 from the court of appeal, State of California, in and for the Third Appellate District and advised by the clerk of the court to return my appellant's opening brief again and appendix that they received on the 30th of January, unfiled. In addition to the time provided by rule 8220 (a)(1) of California rules of the court, appellant was provided two additional opportunities to file a brief in compliance with the requirements of the California rules of the court; my appellant again failed to meet those requirements so therefore, the appeal filed on September 2006 was dismissed.

While working for Pacifica Health/Medical LLC, as a per diem registry nurse throughout the San Diego area, I was informed on

DIVORCE: WHAT AN EDUCATION

the nineteenth of March 2007 that my driver's license as well as my professional nursing license would be suspended effective August 16th due to my lack of payments toward support. After lack of communication, resistance, being threatened with jail time from my ex-wife, her attorney and the court, it wasn't how I do business to resolve this.

I was looking through the yellow pages for an attorney and noticed the name James P. Dunne of Dunne and Dunne LLP, so I made an appointment to meet with him. During our conversation, he wanted to know how he could be of assistance. I explained my legal matter to him as I'd done before with my two previous lawyers; he stated, "This is wrong, I've seen wrong and this is wrong." However, he couldn't do anything about the case because it resided in Sacramento. When I explained the actions of child support, he claimed he would be able to help. He requested all of the documentation from the case, which I provided, and he proposed that we would meet again in two days. When I returned to his office, he was blown away in regards to it and stated, "This is a catastrophe."

Finally, the light bulb flashed on and someone understood what I'd been through and he was more than willing to represent me. Mr. Dunne prepared documentation for order to show cause to prevent the suspension: "On March 19, 2007, I was written a letter informing me that both my driver's license as well as my professional nursing license would be suspended effective August 16, 2007 due to lack of payment of support. I currently work as a registered nurse for Pacifica Health/Medical, LLC. If my nursing license is revoked I will lose my job and will be unable to make any payments of support or arrears whatsoever. The loss of my job would also cause a complete breakdown of my finances. As it stands, I am teetering on the edge of financial ruin. If my nursing license were revoked and I lost my job, I would be unable to survive financially. Therefore, in revoking my nursing license the purpose of the Department of Child Support Services (DCSS) would not be served but instead frustrated. I would be unable to take care of myself financially, much less contribute to the care of the minor children.

My current employment also requires me to have my driver's license. I have to drive to different locations for work. Because I am contracted out, these locations change often and it is vitally important that I have reasonable transportation at my disposal. If my driver's license were revoked, I would be unable to be readily available and flexible as my job requires. I would be susceptible to loss of my job. Again, without my job, I would be unable to support myself, much less anyone less. Therefore, revocation of my driver's license would have a negative impact on my ability to make support payments, not a positive one. Due to the above circumstances, I am requesting a release of my driver's license and nursing license."

Mr. Dunne spent a great deal of time and effort to release the suspension proposed by the DCSS. At the end of June, I was informed that the suspension had been released.

We tried to settle with my ex-wife, but as usual, she was unwilling to compromise or put this to rest. I'd been paying the Department of Child Support Services for many years; however, I received a letter from Mr. Dunne, 2009, advising me that interest on the amount that I owe would no longer continue. But, it still does.

Chapter 5
CHILD SUPPORT

During the settlement conference 2005, the original amount the court set child and spousal support, in 2003, was $5108 and I was ordered to make payments on such amount at a rate of $150 per month.

Ongoing child support was set at $1552 per month and spousal support at $1002 for a total of $2554 monthly. To be in compliance with the support order, my income withheld would be broken down by the following:

- $589.59 weekly
- $ 1,178.77 biweekly (every two weeks)
- $ 1,277.00 semimonthly (twice a month)
- $ 2,554.00 monthly

However, California works by standardized state guidelines, i.e. Disso Master; Disso Master Report is a calculation that will take into consideration the income of both parties, as far as spousal support and including child support. It will also include who

CHILD SUPPORT

has the children what percentage of the time, so time share and income will help determine child support. I was informed that I was a family of four and only had one income so fairness would dictate that seventy five percent of my income would be sent to the three remaining members of the family that weren't working. When my ex-wife obtained gainful employment which would be May or June of 2004, I would be released from spousal support but that never happened.

My ex-wife refused to gain employment and take responsibility for the children when she was advised of my father's illness. I understand the laws about supporting my ex-wife until she completed her nursing degree; however, it changed things when she found a classmate to support her and the kids until she graduated and refused to work, which I believe the court was unaware of. So, it showed that she was unemployed and entitled to all of the support per the court. My income constantly fluctuated over the years working as a travel nurse, but the court ignored every explanation regarding it. My ex-wife explained in her court documentation that she only received two payments: one at the end of 2003 and the other at the beginning of 2004. The checks had derogatory remarks on them showing my hostility and uncooperative behavior such as "I hate u" and "home wrecker." In retrospect, it probably wasn't a good idea because of the repercussions. I have all the receipts from the deposits I made voluntarily to our joint account at $500 a week for six months, in 2003, so her accusations were incorrect in regard to income, especially mine, like most of her documentation presented to the court. Actually, she received an additional $4570.33 per the wage assignment (2004) before I quit my job while in Florida. I was unable to support myself and the dogs because per the above garnishment; child support was taking three quarters of my check. I paid $1900 for the placement of a fence to the property I didn't own for my pets; shortly after this was accomplished, I had to return to California to resolve my legal issues. I was accused of quitting my job and avoiding child support in 2005, which was false. My ex-wife wanted the court to establish the principal support arrearage that I owed and existing order at $1052 per month; as I said, she was only concerned about money. I had a balance of $31,477.67 per child support from the twenty third of September 2003 to the twenty second of September 2005. However, she would waive the interest and penalties if I paid it in ten days. I could only laugh because I should be able to pull that amount out of my ass and settle my debt. The dollar amount had risen that high because I had a meeting with her attorney earlier in the proceedings and he was unwilling to compromise. His last statement was, "We'll get the money one way or the other." I thought to myself if that's how you do business, I won't pay you a dime. My ex mother-in-law stated, "You shouldn't pay her a dime because she doesn't deserve it." Spousal support was set at $1002 per month as I stated; she would agree to a mutual waiver of the spousal support since she did obtain employment as a Registered Nurse, July 2004. Since I hadn't paid any of it, she requested the court establish principal spousal support arrearages in the sum of $24,048 plus interest as accumulated.

Under child support and arrearages in her court documentation of 2005, she wanted the amount be set at $1300 per month for the youngest child and $781 per month for the eldest child for a total of $2084 per month which was incorrect. Remember everything is based on income. When I reopened the case in 2004, I had to provide two months of paystubs for employment per the court; unfortunately, those paystubs showed an increase in my wages related to disasters. During that year, four hurricanes made landfall on the Florida Peninsula; two of them reached land two weeks apart from each other exactly where I was residing at the time. A bad judgment move because I didn't take into account that the court would ignore the reason for the increase.

I had been recalled to the hospital to assist with the care of individuals that were ill or injured from the devastation that had occurred. However, the court didn't want to hear it; they were enforcing judgments based on paystubs alone.

My ex-wife had acquired $9270 in legal fees and costs which had been expanded in attempts to secure and enforce support orders and payments against myself. According to her attorney, my blatant disregard and responsibility to support the children plus my refusal to comply with the court orders, she requested that I be ordered to pay $8000 toward her attorney's fees and costs. I was ordered to pay her attorney fees and costs in the original court documentation September 2003, but it was overlooked based on the advice of my first attorney.

What type of idiot, especially a man, would agree to pay his ex-wife's attorney fees and costs; I made sure that my name was removed from everything that we were connected too and that she paid her own attorney fees and costs. It was the only thing that went in my favor; besides, she was making more money than I was if you took away the disaster pay. As usual, the court didn't see it that way.

All child support payments would continue for each child until further order of the court, the child dies, is emancipated, reaches age nineteen or reaches age eighteen and isn't a full time high school student, whichever comes first. Child support arrearages that I owed were set at $31,477 and interest would continue at a legal rate of ten percent per annum from the first of October 2005 until paid in full. Commencing the first of November 2005, I was ordered to pay $300 per month toward child support arrears until paid in full.

Spousal support arrearages that I owed through September 23, 2005 were set at $24,084 and interest to continue at the legal rate of ten percent per annum as well. However, all collection or enforcement of spousal support arrearages would be suspended so long as I didn't become more than thirty days late on any ongoing monthly child support or child support arrearage payment. So if I became more than 30 days late, my ex-wife could immediately proceed with the collection and enforcement of all child and spousal support arrearages with accumulated interest.

If all child support arrearages paid in full, my ex-wife would agree to forgive and waive the spousal support arrearages in full; that's only if I paid the child support and child support arrearages. Then all ongoing child support orders, obligation would be terminated. Yeah, like that's going to happen.

Child support had the ability to use any collection method authorized under State or Federal Law, including, but not limited, to those methods listed below to collect all past due payments.

- Take your Federal and State refunds which have been received since 2009
- Take any Federal payments owed to you such as tax breaks
- Take any lottery winnings or other money owed to you by the state
- Attach and seize money or assets held by financial institutions

CHILD SUPPORT

1. I had a bank account in California with seventeen dollars in it.
2. Child support got a hold of it and it cost $230 to close it.

- Take a portion of any money owed to you as an independent contractor
- Take a portion of any disability or unemployment benefits
- Take a portion of any personal injury settlements or workman's compensation benefits payments
- Seize any state issued licenses—may be suspended or not renewed
- U.S. Secretary of State may not issue you a passport or may revoke or restrict a current one.

Child support has done everything within their power to ruin my life. For example, I was waiting for my tax return from the government so I could pay my rent at my location outside San Diego 2009; I didn't receive any warning from them. I was broke and had no money to feed my animals so while I was waiting for it; on the fourth of May that year, I had to sell my wedding ring that my mother bought prior to my marriage so I could care for them. A week later, I was informed that child support had intercepted my refund. I called and spoke to a representative of the agency named Sally: I questioned her about seizing my tax return. I told her that I was paying child support and that it was just increased by another sixty dollars, so why did they have to take it? She replied, "We had to do that." I stated to Sally that her mother, meaning my ex-wife's, told me not to pay her a dime when I left because she, my ex-wife's mother, knew that her daughter was wrong. Then, I said, "You have no idea the impact that you are having on the lives of individuals; individuals like myself that you're throwing out onto the street. I'm homeless at the moment." Sally stated, "I'll make a note to your account." I had two words for these people and they weren't pleasant, but I didn't state them.

I had enough money to pay the insurance on my automobile, but started to scramble trying to secure a job quickly; I was able to remain in a hotel room for four days with my dogs. It was difficult to feed them because I barely had enough cash. We were going to be back on the streets by the end of the week, but I was able to find employment through a travel company and we landed in Reno, Nevada.

Child support tried to suspend my drivers and professional licenses which made no sense because if they did that, I wouldn't be able to adhere to my court obligations. They would continually send threatening letters stating the same thing for years; it's a form letter that they send out per their policies and procedures. However, I now receive letters from them when they feel that I'm behind. I send them a payment at the end of a month, but if they don't get it until the following one, I'm behind according to them, which was a bunch of crap. So, I just ignore them because I send my payments and they leave me alone.

At the start of 2006, I had already seen two physicians because of chronic pain in my hips; I had been diagnosed with osteoarthritis years ago and had been struggling and suffering with it for a long time. The X-rays that I had done in December 2005 showed severe end stage osteoarthritis with subluxation of the hip. Your hip is a ball and socket joint, so subluxation means that the ball is behind the socket.

I made an appointment with Dr. John Dearborn, an

orthopedic surgeon located at the Washington Hospital in Fremont, California at the Joint Replacement Center. His specialty was replacing knees and hips so I was advised that my left leg was five inches shorter than my right when I was examined by him. I made arrangements to have surgery.

I told my second attorney my intentions and that we needed to petition the court for a modification of child support and arrears determination. Judge McBrien wasn't going to make any modifications in child support until we provided proof that the surgery took place, how long I would be out of work and what income I would have while recovering from the surgery.

Judge McBrien was well aware of Dr. Dearborn and his microscopic surgery where the patients are up and walking in two days. When I went to court on the tenth of May, the judge noted that Dr. Dearborn is well known for the quick recovery of his patients and their ability to return to work. It was a different judge at the time, but he knew of Dr. Dearborn as well. When I was questioned about the surgery, I told the court that everyone is an individual and that some people take longer to heal; I was given a two-week grace period from paying child and spousal support.

It's ironic because years later, I learned that Judge McBrien had one of his hips replaced as well.

With the help of my third attorney, I was able to prevent the suspension and revoking of my drivers and professional licenses as I've already stated. But my lawyer requested that the Department of Child Support Services conduct an audit to determine the actual arrears I owed.

I was informed by my attorney's office on the eleventh of April 2008 in regard to my current income, that it seemed higher at this point than it was at the date of the order; it's possible that a request for modification of support may cause the payment to increase or not decrease. This was even more likely given the fact that my lawyer believed that my ex-wife earned around the same as she did at the date of the judgment. With that in mind, he recommended removing a modification request from the proceedings as well as minimizing monthly payments because it's based on my income. Child support could turn around and file for modification of the support to increase monthly payments; the $88 difference in arrears payments wasn't enough of a detriment to take such a risk.

My ex-wife sent a request to my attorney in San Diego the twenty eighth of January 2009, to have my child support order reviewed. As a result, my child support order would be reviewed to see if the amount in the order should be changed. As I always said, my ex-wife was all about money. If I didn't return the requested form(s) within twenty days from the date of the letter, child support would proceed with the review based on the information that my ex-wife provided which, as we know, would be false. I had to complete the form(s) as quickly as possible, then I wrote them a note. I told them it didn't matter what information I provided because Child Support Services continued to enforce the rules and regulations of the agency upon me without allowing me the opportunity to respond. Besides, they were just as biased toward women as the court; maybe if they walked a mile in the shoes of these individuals, like myself, they would have some compassion and empathy. They would understand that something is wrong, but I've been told that the agency doesn't care.

I didn't get the notification until the sixth of February, and they would probably ignore my input. My ex-wife has portrayed herself as the victim in this legal matter and manipulated not only

CHILD SUPPORT

child support, but the court as well. Instead of having any regard for the children, she went out and found another man to take care of her.

I was advised by child support that my ex-wife didn't complete and return the required income and expenses forms or required documents. So, it was never acted upon.

Over the years, I made offers to my ex-wife to settle this legal matter, but she was unwilling. I offered to pay $1000 a month for the eldest child until she turns eighteen and $500 for the youngest until she reaches the same age plus pay her $24,000 in arrears. It was turned down. Next, I offered to pay child support for the youngest child because the eldest was eighteen and $50,000 in arrears, but my ex-wife wasn't willing to work out any type of agreement unless it benefitted her.

My last attorney prepared a statement on my behalf to offer my ex-wife a lump sum of $5000 as a payment in full of arrearages owed; she refused.

Many individuals, from friends to family, stated that I should get another attorney, but I wasn't going to do that. Instead, I looked at several fathers' rights groups and basically, there's nothing that can be done; I don't receive my Federal and State Income tax refunds, so I claim exempt on my W-2 forms. I might have to pay a little more at the end of the year; however, if I don't get my return, she doesn't either.

Recently, I received a letter from the Sacramento County Department of Child Support Services (SCDCSS) advising that I have spousal support arrears open with their office; they were writing to inform me of an upcoming change to it. SCDCSS doesn't receive funding, and thus is not required to enforce spousal support orders unless there is an ongoing child support obligation, such as custody. Therefore, in the following situation, SCDCSS would no longer enforce spousal support:

- There is only a medical support order for the child (ren)
- There is a zero child support order - The child support issue is reserved
- There are child support arrears (past due support), but no ongoing child support obligation

Because I had no current child support obligation, SCDCSS would no longer enforce spousal support and spousal support arrears are no longer owed. This change didn't mean that spousal support or spousal support arrears were no longer owed. It simply meant the order(s) would not be enforced by SCDCSS. As of the twenty eighth of February 2014, SCDCSS records show that I owe a total of $44,282.75 in spousal support arrears approximately. I forwarded this letter to my third attorney hoping that I could get his interpretation on this matter because I just didn't understand it.

I was able to reach my attorney's office and spoke to James Dunne's paralegal assistant, Jeanette. She wasn't able to interpret the letter I received from the SCDCSS. I was advised that the office would have to petition the court to retrieve the file and would have to review it before any course of action was warranted. However if I wanted to pursue the meaning of the letter, there would be a $2000 retainer fee for my attorney's services which I couldn't afford. On the contrary, I received another letter from the SCDCSS on the sixteenth of June 2014. It was my monthly billing statement showing the balance I owe in child support. I was surprised because the total interest and principal balance

CHILD SUPPORT

was $50,984.24. So, spousal support was removed from the total amount, which was more than $49,000. But SCDCSS continues to apply interest to this amount that was supposed to cease in 2009.

Chapter 6
SINGLE PARENTS

A single parent is a parent not living with a spouse or partner, who has most of the day to day responsibilities in raising the child or children. A single parent is usually considered the primary caregiver, meaning the parent and children have residency a majority of the time. If the parents are separated or divorced, children live with their custodial parent and have visitation or secondary residence with the non-custodial parent. In Western society, following separation, a child will reside with the primary caregiver, usually the mother, and a secondary caregiver, usually the father.

Historically, death of a partner was a major cause of single mothers or single parenting. Single mothers or single parenting can result from separation, death, child abuse/neglect, or divorce of a couple with children. Custody battles, awarded by the court or rationalized in other terms, determine who the child will spend a majority of their time with; this affects children in many ways and counseling is suggested for them. A mother is typically the primary caregiver in a single parent family structure because of divorce or unplanned pregnancy. Fathers have been less common primary caregivers in the past, presumably due to working most of the day, resulting in less bonding with the children, possibly a young child still needing to nurse, or if childcare was necessary while fathers work, so the mother would be better suited while fathers worked. The scenario has shifted in recent years as many fathers are taking an active parental role as a stay-at-home dad as more mothers are in the workforce and being the sole provider to the family, resulting in fathers bonding and connecting more to their children. Single-mother or single-parent-adoption is sometimes an option for adults who want children but don't want to have a partner.

Demographics of single parenting show a general increase worldwide in children living in single parent homes. Single parenting has become an accepted norm in the United States and a trend found in multiple other countries. Debates concerning not only single parents themselves but the children involved, support for the families in single parent households, and more have arisen. Although divorce is one of the main events that leads to single mothers and parenting, it may be that the majority of cases in the United States are from pregnancy outside of wedlock.

Single mothers or parenthood has been common historically due to high parental mortality rate (due to disease, wars and maternal mortality). Historical estimates indicate that in French, English, or Spanish villages in the seventieth and eighteenth centuries, at least one third of children lost their parents during childhood. In the nineteenth century Milan, about half of all children lost at least one parent by age twenty while in China, almost one third of boys had lost one parent or both by age fifteen. Divorce was generally rare historically (although this depends upon culture and era), and divorce especially became very difficult to obtain after the fall of the Roman Empire in Medieval Europe, due to strong involvement of ecclesiastical courts in family life through annulment and other more common forms of separation.

In the early years of the Roman Empire, the woman had little power: they were expected to be mothers and run household tasks. Infertility was grounds from divorce. Women didn't have a choice between having children or not and were not able to overrule the husband if he wanted to get rid of the newborn. After birth, babies were placed at the father's feet; if he picked the child up, he recognized it as his but if he left it where it was, the child was left to die by exposure. Later, as women gained economic power, Roman Empire mothers exercised a genuine influence over family decisions.

In Medieval times, the diet was low in iron which women needed more than men. Iron deficiencies meant many women died much earlier than men but if they survived their childbearing years, they often lived longer than men. Later, a woman's life expectancy was significantly raised with change in agriculture that brought better nutrition. Women generally had four to six pregnancies over the course of twenty childbearing years but a high rate of miscarriages and still births. Women were either pregnant or nursing for most of their adult lifespan. Up until the eighteenth century, twenty-five percent of children born in England died in their first year. For women of all social classes, raising a son to adulthood was the only means of securing their own support in old age.

Motherhood in early modern times has been described as nasty, brutish and far from short. Like Medieval women, early modern women spent about fifteen years either pregnant or nursing their children. Peasant mothers would hang their swaddled babies on hooks to keep them out of the way while the woman performed an exhausting number of daily chores. Babies were also carried out to the fields and placed near where their mothers worked, sometimes secured in trees.

The Reformation was key in upgrading motherhood to a teaching position. Protestantism held that mothers were expected to read the Bible to their children and to instruct their children in reading and religious knowledge. Of course, women were still restricted from official positions in the church and many women in lower social classes remained illiterate, but the foundations of women as educators were laid.

While motherhood usually refers to direct personal care aspects of mothering, the woman's ability to contribute to the income of the household can be considered a form of motherhood. So, it's natural to expect that an economic force like the Industrial Revolution would reshape the role and perception of motherhood. The effect of the Industrial Revolution on women's employment was mixed. On the positive side, some claim that new labor opportunities developed. However, with limitation for women (legal and otherwise), the classic division between the man as a provider and woman as domestic expert began. Working class families needed to pool wages to survive would tend to bear more children to have as many working hands as possible.

In the U.S., the 1930s marked a radical shift in family structure and the ideals of family life. A good mother didn't work; women who did pursue careers were stigmatized as selfish, devoid of proper maternal instinct and nature. The Great Depression only furthered the need for a mother to keep the family together while the man was out trying to provide for his family. The role

DIVORCE: WHAT AN EDUCATION

of mothers became even more crucial and demanding during the 1940s, because husbands and sons went off to war. The war years caused most families incredible hardship. Around five million war widows were left alone to cook, clean, and care for the children. Women made up for the workforce lost overseas, trying to hold down factory jobs which demanded long hours. Stresses and strains of separation, along with war trauma, caused a spike in the divorce rate after the war.

Marriage and birth rates soared at the end of the war and women were again placed in charge of housekeeping and raising the family. The 1950s encouraged the ideal of a "stable and model" family. The American Dream: Ray H. Abrams's article, "The Concept of Family Stability" (November 1950), emphasizes the materialistic bent of this dream: "the ideal family" raising its standards of living by security, better homes, automobiles, education, radio and television sets, along with fashion in an attempt to climb the social ladder.

The sexual revolution of the 1960s allowed women to begin to exert power and freedom more publicly. Despite the revolution and the efforts of minority groups to gain equal rights, attitudes toward women changed surprisingly little. Most American women in the '60s were mothers and housewives volunteering at churches and PTAs. Business and politics remained almost exclusively controlled by men. Women did start to work more outside the home, but those who did were still in the minority. In a huge leap forward for women's choice in having children, the 1960s saw the birth control pill become widely available to the public with 1.2 million American women taking the pill by 1962.

Two point three million were on the pill by 1963, and by 1965, 6.5 million women were taking it.

SINGLE PARENTS

The most significant changes in women's roles were brought about by the rise in feminism in the 1960s and 1970s. Women organized for equal rights, and employment finally began to change. Women with college degrees were actually using those degrees to enter the professional world. Children as young as two and three years old were sent to preschools, allowing mothers to pursue careers as well as have a family. Notably, Susan Douglas and Meredith argue in *The Mommy Myth* that media since the 1970s has created an impossible to reach idealized mother figure that has subtly demonized the working mother's role, her attention away from the perfect mom details coming off as unduly sacrificed. Women and mothers in general are certainly working more, while under a third of married women worked outside the home in 1961. By the 1990s, closer to two thirds of married women were in paid employment in 1961. In 1991, it was over half. As wages have trended toward equality, more and more cases of the typically maternal role have shifted to men as part of a greater redefining of the women's and mother's place in society. Single motherhood is more accepted, women have more rights, and while domestic arrangement stereotypes still exist, they are on the decline.

Since the 1960s in the United States, there has been a marked increase in the number of children living with a single parent. The 1960s United States Census reported that nine percent of children were dependent on a single parent, a number that has increased by twenty-eight percent by the 2000 U.S. Census.

The spike was caused by an increase in births to unmarried women and the prevalence of divorces among couples. In 2010, 40.7 percent of births in the U.S. were to unmarried women. In 2000, 11 percent of children were living with parents who had never been married, 15.6 percent of children lived with a divorced parent and 1.2 percent lived with a parent who was widowed. The results of the 2010 United States Census showed that 27 percent of children live with one parent, consistent with the emerging trend noted in 2000.

About 16 percent of children worldwide live in a single parent household. In 2006, 12.9 million families in the U.S. were headed by a single parent, 80 percent of which were headed by a female. In 2003, 14 percent of all Australian households were single parent families. In 2010, 34 percent of children born in Australia were born to unmarried women. In the United Kingdom, about one out of four families with dependent children are single parent homes; 8 to 11 percent of which have a male single parent. UK poverty figures show that 52 percent of single parent families are below the government defined poverty line after housing costs. Countries located in Asia and the Middle East are the least likely to have children raised in single parent households. On the other hand, the three areas of the world that are most likely to have non marital childbearing are Latin America, South Africa, and Sweden. Along with this, the areas where there are an extremely high number of children living in single parent households include Africa, Europe, Latin America, North America, and Oceania. According to the New York Times, how a single parent is defined is dependent on each individual country's culture. In the United Stated, 80.6 percent of single parents are mothers and among this percentage of single mothers 45 percent of them are currently divorced or separated, 1.7 percent are widowed, and 34 percent never have been married. The prevalence of single mothers as primary caregivers is a part of traditional parenting trends between mothers and fathers. In her work Marriage and Families,

SINGLE PARENTS

Nijole V. Benokraitis, Ph.D in sociology conducted research with marriage, family and gender roles. She defines mothers as the expressive role players who provide the emotional support and nurturing that sustain the family unit. She argues that mothers outshine fathers who tend to be stricter and more distant; children tend to drift toward preference of parent depending on how involved a particular parent is and a common problem in society today are absentee fathers; therefore, children are more likely a definition of a mother's role. Also the preferences of the mother because of their protective nurturing characteristics from a long established mother child relationship from early attachment, beginning at birth and continuing as the child grows up.

Today, there are nearly 13.6 million single parents raising over 21,000,000 children. Single fathers are far less common than single mothers, constituting 16 percent of single parent families. According to Single Parent Magazine, the number of single fathers has increased by 60 percent in the last ten years and is one of the fastest growing family situations in the United States. Sixty percent of single fathers are divorced, by far the most common cause of this family situation. In addition, there is an increasing trend of men having children through surrogates and raising them alone. While fathers aren't normally seen as primary caregivers, statistics show 905 persons of single fathers are employed and 72 percent have a full time job.

"Fathers" have been variously defined throughout history as provider, demanding, disciplinarian, and even cruel. Yet, as the writer Armstong Williams remarks in the article "The Definition of Father" ... every father must take the time to be a dad as well as a friend, disciplinarian, shoulder to cry on, dance partner, coach, audience, adviser, listener, and so much more." Williams, the writer quoted above, goes on to say that he viewed his father as the driving force in his family and someone who brought strength and compassion to his family. In addition to these qualities, the single father must take on the role of the mother; a role that extends deep into morality, devotion, and the ability to set up an educational yet nurturing environment. Thus, it is the father's role to be a source of both resilience, strength, love, and compassion. There has been little specific research regarding the positives of the father as a single parent; however, there are various proven pros that accompany single parenting. One proven statistic about single fathers states that a single father tends to use more positive parenting techniques than a married father. As far as nonspecific pros, a strong bond tends to be formed between parent and child in a single parenting situation.

In 2009, the overall divorce rate was around nine out of a thousand in the United States; it was also found that more influence came from the South, with the rates there being about ten point five out of thousand, as opposed to the north where it was around seven out of a thousand. This resulted in about one point five percent (around 1 million) of children living in the home of recently divorced parents in the same year. Over the past ten years or so, first marriages have a fifty percent chance of ending in divorce and for other marriages after the first divorce, the chance of another divorce increased.

Tom Leykis is an American talk radio personality best known for hosting The Tom Leykis Show from 1994 to 2009 (nationally syndicated) and April 2012 to the present (internet stream cast/podcast). The show follows Hot Talk format which brought Leykis much success, particularly in the Southern California radio market. Due to the provocative nature of the show, Leykis

SINGLE PARENTS

has often been described as a shock jock. The show's best known feature is "Leykis 101," in which he purports to teach men "how to get laid" while spending the least amount of time, money, and effort.

The cornerstone of the program is the Thursday broadcast of "Leykis 101" in which the program is set up as an ad hoc lecture, question and answer session where he presides as a self-styled "professor." The subject of the "101" segments are how men can spend less money on women while achieving greater sexual and personal success. The intent of his advice is to serve as a "father figure" for his mostly male listeners many of whom were raised without a father. Thus, many callers address Leykis as "Dad" or "Father."

Along with general information on life for young men, Leykis's 101 advice mostly consists of his principles of looking out for oneself. He argues that the institution of marriage is flawed and that "family court" systems are often corrupt because DNA testing after childbirth is not mandatory to prevent "paternity fraud" and the courts have forced men to pay "child support" even after DNA testing has established that a man was not actually a child's father. Other examples of Leykis 101 guidelines included "never dating a single mother" or coworkers, never cohabiting with a woman, use "birth control" during each sexual encounter and immediately end a relationship if a woman issues an ultimatum.

Leykis constantly recommends that young men pursue their career or educational goals and not be distracted by serious relationships or marriage at a young age as he was. Leykis describes many women as "dream killers" (i.e., he argues that in dating or marriage women will typically prioritize their desires above a man's and will actively discourage a man's ambitions for fear of

DIVORCE: WHAT AN EDUCATION

him leaving the relationship if he attains success.) Furthermore, Leykis urges men to live frugally, including avoiding consumer debt (what Leykis describes as "renting money"); never spending more than forty dollars for a date and saving cash for investing in the future. He has described men who neglect their bills as "immoral."

When I learned about Tom Leykis and his radio talk show, it was too late. The very things he preached I did, such as living with my ex-wife for a year, getting married, adopting her children, being released from the family unit, and not adhering to verbal clues. For example, my ex-wife stated early in our relationship that she wanted someone to take care of her and her children, which I ignored.

However, the Leykis Show taught young men how they can spend less money on women while achieving greater sexual and personal success. He would also teach women what men were like so they didn't fall into the pitfalls with them.

His last broadcast on the radio was the 20th of February 2009, but returned on his podcast/stream cast network," The New Normal Network "at 3:00 p.m. Pacific time, on the 2nd of April 2012 was one day after his CBS contract ended. The new uncensored show includes a new theme song, fewer commercials, and "Leykis 101" news at the top of the hour.

For young men and women, the Tom Leykis Show might be a resource for future decisions in regard to members of the opposite sex.

Recently on social media, there was a dating site to meet single mothers; I plan to avoid that application.

Chapter 7
CHILDREN

At the beginning of 1999, I took residence with my ex-wife and her children. She stated that I should get to know them first and become their friend because she had been both parents, which included being the disciplinarian for the kids. The youngest was confused and needed an explanation from my ex-wife so she could understand the situation.

Jennifer Lopez, who played Mary Fiore in the movie, "The Wedding Planner," saw her father's marriage to her mother as being perfect. On the contrary, her father, Salvatore, portrayed by Alex Rocco, revealed that his wedding to her mother was actually arranged and only became a loving relationship months later. Her father explained that he had fallen ill and her mother took care of him so they began to like each other. Then, he said like turned into respect and respect grew into love. I did the same thing with the children.

The girls immediately took to my cat that I left with them so they could enjoy and care for him as an ice breaker; unfortunately, their mother was allergic to him, so I had to give him away and they were sad. But, we acquired a couple of dogs later.

I had a wonderful relationship with the girls because they so desperately needed a male figure. It's a documented fact that children, 85 percent, do better after a divorce when the father has sole or joint custody (*No BS Strategies Divorce for Men*.) Children suffer when restricted to limited contact with their father, whether biological or stepparent.

Initially, the girls were spending time between their parents every other weekend each month.

I had been with my ex-wife and the children for approximately nine months before we started the process of having them adopted so they could have a steady and healthy environment. It was a long process because of dealing with the biological father who didn't make it easy. My ex-wife and I spent at least two to three times a week in court, which has been documented because of the biological father's lies, fabrications, and his attempt to get me removed from the family unit. Also, he was detrimental to them, as I stated numerous times, because he would fill their heads with all kinds of promises and dreams that would not come true. For example, he told the youngest that if she came to live with him, she would be able to ride a pony to school every day. He wouldn't agree to a mutual meeting place for the exchange of the girls and sometimes, he would only return one of them and not the other. Their mother had told stories about when the minors were eight and six; they went to visit their father in Alaska. However when they were scheduled to be returned, they were nowhere to be found and were missing for three months. The children even appeared on milk cartons back in the day. Eventually, they were returned. Two years later, the family court ordered the minors to once again be able to visit their father for a three-week vacation, but they were only returned after their mother contacted the district attorney's office. When the children were with the father, he would ask general questions to them and, unknowingly, they would just answer them. However, he was trying to extort information about my ex-wife and myself. This information he would try to use in Court. The biological father constantly petitioned the court that he was being denied seeing his children, he had little or no contact with them and when the children reached out to him, there was no response. At one point during this process, their father stated to them that he wouldn't see them anymore and the children had no further contact with him since Halloween of 1999. The children were coming of age and they wanted to spend most of their time with friends; they didn't want to visit their father as deemed by the court.

Dealing with the biological father and the ongoing process to adopt the children, they needed to be interviewed so the Petition for Adoption could be approved by the court (2002). Per family law in the State of California, the views, opinions, and decisions would be heard if the minor was 14 years old. At the time of the interview, the oldest child was of this age. She indicated that she had a good school year and just graduated from the eighth grade. She would be enrolled in high school in the fall and had been accepted onto the cheerleading squad. She stated that she had a 3.5 grade point average throughout the school year and was looking forward to school in the fall because of her excellent grades at school. She was keeping the pet chinchilla from her science class for the summer. When she was asked about her hobbies, she stated that she enjoys talking on the phone, hanging out with her friend, and practicing her cheerleading. During the school year, the eldest won a science award and became interested in becoming a micro- biologist in the future. She thought that I was a really good guy, like a father to her and she liked that. She stated, "he loves and spoils us rotten." We would go to the movies, watch television and spend time at the Family Fun Center. At the Family Fun Center, we would shoot water balloons at each other and see who would get wet. The oldest child didn't really remember anything about her father; however, when she went to visit a few years ago, she recalls her father leaving the house or drinking alcoholic beverages. During another visit, she cut her foot on a broken glass bottle that had contained alcohol; but at times, she felt like his maid because she would have to watch his other children while he was at work. When asked if there was anything she wanted the court to know about her opinion on the adoption, the eldest stated, "I think it's a good idea and I like it."

Next, the youngest, who was twelve years old, was interviewed; she stated that she just graduated from the sixth grade and was looking forward to entering junior high. She believed that she had a good school year and enjoyed history and reading; her hobbies were dancing and cheerleading. She was very excited because she'd recently been accepted onto the community cheerleading squad. The minor child and I would go camping, to amusement parks, or just talk a lot; she was always able to express herself when we were together. She stated that I cared, supported, and loved her and she wanted to be adopted. She stated, "not a lot" in regard to remembering anything about her father.

They were good kids even though they spent most of their lives in a broken home. I never played favorites and treated them equally. If I was out in town with one of the girls and they wanted something, I made sure we got something for the other. Our goal was to keep the girls out of trouble because so many kids these

CHILDREN

days get involved with the wrong type of individuals. So, we kept them busy with dance lessons, cheerleading and beauty pageants. They won awards. For example, the eldest was Miss Orangevale 2001 and the youngest was Miss Loomis that same year for their respective age groups during the beauty pageants they entered in those towns just north of Sacramento, California.

However, it was a difficult time for the children when I left at the end of 2002; I learned that the eldest child cried all day. Unfortunately, their lives didn't get any better; in fact, it got worse. Maybe their lives would have been better if they'd remained at my side, but you don't know.

The older child was very popular in school, always had a boyfriend, was homecoming queen, and a cheerleader; but I always stressed that she needed to take care of herself first. I meant that she needed to get her education and everything else would fall into place, especially boys. I told her as I heard the echoes of my father, "It will be your time." I told her that on several occasions, but she took a different path. I was called upon her during the marriage for advice and briefly after we separated because she was looking for a male perspective on any subject. If she had a question concerning sex, she would seek my advice; I remember sitting around the kitchen table with her and a group of her girlfriends talking about it.

I tried to remain in contact with the children after their mother and I went our separate ways, but it was difficult. Every correspondence, phone conversation, and visitation with them was presented to the court by their mother. For example, I had the youngest child visit when I was still living in California; of course, I had no assistance from my ex-wife with transportation. When I was unable to return the child in a timely manner because I had

DIVORCE: WHAT AN EDUCATION

to work; I advised her. However, it didn't matter because it appeared in the court documentation.

My ex-wife made every effort to show the court that I wasn't spending nearly enough time with the children. For example, the children wanted to visit Florida after I returned there, in 2004, to support my parents. However, I had paid for everything in order to see them. I paid over $600 in air fare, entertained them, and paid for any souvenirs because their mother didn't send them with any money; she expected that it was my responsibility to do all of that.

The eldest came first, but I wasn't told by her or her mother that she went to the doctor because of having back and flank pain. So, she was given a prescription for pain and a urine sample was never obtained. Two days after her arrival, the eldest was complaining of being nauseous, vomiting, back pain, and was pale. Unfortunately, I had to admit her to the hospital with a kidney infection, better known as pyelonephritis.

I didn't get much sleep during those days because of taking her back and forth to the hospital where I obtained gainful employment after my return to Florida. I worked nights and would visit her before my shift and before she went to bed. In the morning, I returned to her room and sat in the chair waiting for her to wake up.

A few days later, the youngest arrived; she was delayed because of a hurricane. I took both of them to several places and they enjoyed their time once her sister was released from the hospital. The hospital sent a statement for the medical cost for her admission and it was over $6000; however, it was reduced by $2000 because I worked at the facility. Not to mention, $165 for the hospital admit and discharge. Also, $550 in physician fees and

CHILDREN

$385 for laboratory testing. The last time I saw the children was at the end of the year 2004 as mentioned.

During the settlement conference in 2005, my ex-wife requested that I pay for the medical expenses she acquired for the children and had no intentions of providing any financial contribution to any of the medical cost I had obtained, even though she achieved her nursing degree in July of 2004 and found gainful employment. Since I paid all of the medical costs for the eldest child, she was made to pay the cost she required because I wasn't.

I always thought of the children over the years and how their lives turned out. Six years passed before I was able to make contact with them again. While residing in California (2010), I was able to locate the oldest child via social media. When I joined the website, I made one statement to her, "I still have the dogs." She immediately knew who I was and responded. She mentioned and I quote, "What the hell happened to you? You were in our lives then disappeared." I explained to her the difficulty of remaining in contact and she understood.

We spoke on several occasions and I learned that she had led a troubled life. According to her, she claimed that her mother would constantly hit her and that she would get hit when her younger sister did something that their mother disapproved of. She mentioned that her mother punched her in the face during a fight and then she left. She was followed by an automobile, but saved by a friend. She couldn't wait to turn eighteen and get out from her mother's control; however, she didn't listen to my advice about taking care of herself. She revealed that she was a recovering drug addict and was in recovery for the second time but unable to reside with her mother because her mother was taking pain killers for which she had an addiction. She stated, that her mother" would go to work doped up on them." While in recovery, she met a young man that was there for the first time; they struck up a relationship and resided in a house that was provided by her new boyfriend's father. The young man worked for his father and wanted to be responsible for taking care of my daughter and granddaughter. As I said, she always had a boyfriend. However, she'd had a child out of wedlock with another man, though the relationship didn't last because he was emotionally and verbally abusive to her. She nearly died during childbirth but survived and they worked out a schedule so each of them could spend time with their daughter because she didn't want to enter a custody battle similar to the one with her biological father. She had been there herself as a child. She expressed her concerns about the relationship because of being unhappy. She thought it wasn't working, was one-sided, and she was the one holding it together. She felt her current boyfriend had no motivation. It was evident during the holidays of 2010 when I went to visit her with the dogs that she was happy to see them again, because they were a part of her life for a brief period of time. When I first saw her, she thought that I had changed. I stated, "I'm the same guy that I ever was." We had several conversations about her relationship and I gave my advice to help her. I bought groceries and gave her some cash too. After I left, she decided to leave her boyfriend so she could turn her life around for the better; however, she couldn't leave her current location because of the biological father with whom she had a child. So, she remained in a hotel room with my support, but I learned later that she was spending time with her former boyfriend whom she'd left. Her boyfriend was playing on her emotions, telling her that he couldn't live without her and attempted suicide twice. Fortunately, the eldest child was there both

CHILDREN

times to save his life. But, his father thought my daughter wasn't good enough for his son even though he showed very little gratitude for her efforts. After everything that they had been through, they got engaged and were soon to be married, but his father wasn't consenting and gave his son an ultimatum; they opted to leave. They were sleeping in the car and at the house of friends. Shortly after that, I received a text from her that he'd found another woman, wanted the engagement ring back, and she was left on the street. She verbalized that she had sold everything and now stood on the street corner panhandling for money. Plus, she lost the granddaughter to the man that fathered her child and only had visitation rights. She constantly called asking for money because of the possibility of returning to jail on charges related to her past. She had been in jail twice convicted on felony charges. The first time, she was pregnant and scared that the Mexican girls were going to beat her up; however, the second time was better because she was remembered. I sent her $150 and then lost contact with her again.

She was such a bright child, had so much potential, and could have done anything with her life once she applied herself. Her goal was to return to school and become a pastry chef because she loved to bake. She wanted to be like the Cake Boss, a series on the television learning channel (TLC). I told her I would quit my job and come work for her; she was excited that I would make such a statement. She was attempting to retrieve her driver's license because it had been revoked and it would cost $500. Once she regained that privilege, she was going to purchase a vehicle from her mother that she doesn't drive (because she owned five of them). She said that it wasn't my fault the marriage between her mother and I didn't work after she had the opportunity to read

DIVORCE: WHAT AN EDUCATION

all of the court documentation when her mother went to Hawaii. She thought her mother was having an affair on her current husband during her visit. She discovered all of the military items that belonged to her father and was planning to return them to him; I told her that she should because you only get to experience the military once and you'll never be able to get those items back that you've obtained during the time spent in the service. She agreed.

The family had turned their backs on her because of her past, but I would always listen and assist her as much as I could. I mentioned to her that her life would have been better if we stayed together, but her reply was, "You don't know that."

I was on social media and discovered that she had passed away, so I decided to investigate this fact a little further. Her passing occurred on the 10th of April, in Marysville, California, 2012. The police called it one of the worst wrecks in recent memory and one of the worst traffic collisions they had in quite a while because of the number of victims and the amount of damaged property.

She was standing at the corner of F and 10th Street; one report states the northwest corner and the other the southwest; however, a Jeep Commander North of F Street crossed the southbound land and drove up on the sidewalk. The vehicle hit and killed her instantly, injuring several others that were taken to local hospitals and one person airlifted to a trauma center. The Jeep Commander continued, hitting a signal control light box and a telephone pole, splitting it in half; the intersection was littered with broken car parts, splintered wood, wrapped metal and broken glass scattered over a surprisingly large area. More than 2,200 residents of Marysville were without power for about thirty minutes following the crash. Then, the Commander hit the passenger side of an eastbound Kia Rio, which was stopped at a traffic light. The Jeep

CHILDREN

landed on its driver's side on the center island of 10th Street and the Kia Rio came to rest on F Street north of 10th. Three weeks prior to this deadly accident, the police conducted a speed enforcement operation from the 10th Street Bridge to F Street and recorded speeds up to 91 mph. However, they were just urging people to slow down and drive at safer speeds. The police believed that she was standing at the northwest corner with the young man she met in recovery, when the collision occurred. I had his phone number, but lost contact with her; I didn't know they were still together. I couldn't believe what I read and saw from the video; it was incredible. The celebration of her life was held at Chapel of the Pines Funeral Home in Placerville, California on the 17th of April, but I was unable to attend. I gained access to images of the ceremony. She had been cremated and her remains were placed on a table surrounded with flowers and pictures of her which were beautiful. She was only twenty-four years old when she passed and trying to straighten out her life from all the turmoil that occurred. But I was included in her life, no matter what the circumstances were, and I was always there to assist her when I was able.

As far as the youngest goes, her sister told a story about how her mother once grabbed her by the throat and slammed her against the wall, even though her mother stated that she would never hit her children. This was a lie. Prior to the death of her sister, I was able to contact her. I already knew that the youngest child had an argument with her mother, packed up with a young man and moved to Pennsylvania just outside a small town from her biological father. She was extremely difficult to reach because of the time zone difference and was very busy attending classes for cosmetology. She wanted to open her own salon one day but has the responsibility for four children.

The youngest was very introverted and shy, but would always be able to talk about anything when we were together. I remember one time she verbalized that the kids in school were mean to her because she had a lot of hair on her arms so I would shave them because she had complete trust in me instead of her mother. When I left the family unit, the eldest stated that her mother thought her sister needed psychiatric counseling which wasn't necessary because her mother constantly had men rotating in and out of her life. I don't have much contact with the youngest—just on occasion with social media—because she has her own life as I explained.

The statements made by the eldest child cannot be denied or confirmed because she's gone and they would not be permissible in a court of law. She would speak the truth and always had the confidence to reveal what she was thinking, feeling, and events happening or those that did happen.

Chapter 8
THE LION DOG

What can I say about man's best friend? - You guessed it - it's a dog. During our marriage, we acquired two Shih Tzu's; first, a male then six months later a female. History of the Shih Tzu dates back thousands of years ago and this breed is one of the oldest of all dogs. The Shih Tzu has its origins in Tibet and China; however, there's a long-standing controversy because some say the dog originated in China, whereas others say it originated in Tibet. The most popular belief is that the earliest form of the Shih Tzu came from Tibet and then was introduced to China; however, due to breed changes throughout the centuries, the modern day Shih Tzu is best related to being Chinese.

The Shih Tzu breed, as we know it today, was developed in the seventeenth century by crossing the Lhasa Apso and Pekingese and these dogs were highly favored by Chinese royalty, so they were kept on the palace grounds for decades. They were so prized that the Chinese refused to sell or trade these dogs until the 1930s.

The word "shih tzu" means 'lion' and this is exactly why the Chinese loved this animal. Before Communism, when Buddhism

DIVORCE: WHAT AN EDUCATION

was widespread, a lion was the spiritual and symbolic ideal for both Chinese and Tibetans. Shih Tzu dogs were actually bred to resemble lions and were considered holy; thus, they inherited the name "Lion Dog." There's a Shih Tzu urban legend that surrounds them which claims that these dogs were kept by Buddhist Monks in temples for thousands of years. Manjusri, one of Buddhists' spiritual figures known as their god of learning, used to carry a small dog with him which he called the Lion Dog because it looked like a miniature lion. As the legend goes, this little dog would transform into a real life-size lion and carry Manjusri on his back. Even though this is quite a stretch of imagination, it's obvious that tales such as this one contributed to the popularity and fame of these dogs in China and Tibet.

The exact date of origin for the Shih Tzu is not known, but evidence of its existence has come from documents, paintings, and object d'art dating from 624 A.D. during the Tang Dynasty (618 - 907 A. D.). The King of Viqur gave the Chinese court a pair of dogs said to have come from the FU Lin (assumed to be the Byzantine Empire.) It's known that the Shih Tzu was a house pet during most of the Ming Dynasty (1368- 1644 A.D.) and highly favored by the royal family.

The first person in recent memory to record Shih Tzu history was the Dowager Empress Tzu HSI who ruled China in the mid– 1800s. According to records, she bred these dogs to develop specific attributes and characteristics. One of the strongest characteristics of the Shih Tzu was its personality. They are friendly, non-aggressive dogs that are good companions for children and other breeds of dog. They are also known for their fun-loving play, romping around the apartment or in the countryside.

The Shih Tzu's are people-oriented dogs, they cherish nothing more than the love of people. They will sit patiently remaining still with their eyes gazing intently on your face, waiting for you to call them over to be petted. The Shih Tzu is not a one-person dog; they are happy to entertain any stranger once accepted by the family. This is one reason that they are becoming popular and make friends wherever they go. The Shih Tzu has a lap dog personality, not high strung nor demanding and content during the day to lie in a corner with its legs stretched out behind it, snoring softly. If they had a choice they would prefer to be curled up in your lap. In addition to breeding the Shih Tzu, she (Dowager Empress Tzu HSI) also bred Pekingese dogs and Pugs. However, after her death, her dogs were sold, bred throughout China and were exported to the West.

Shih Tzus were first introduced to England and Norway in the 1930s; however, they were first classified as being "APSOS" by the Kennel Club. It wasn't until 1935 that these dogs became known as Shih Tzus and their breed was standardized by England's Shih Tzu Club. Then after World War II, American soldiers found the Shih Tzu and returned to the United States with a few. These dogs soon got a new "nickname" by Westerners i.e., The Chrysanthemum Dog. They were thusly named as their fur grew outwards on their face, which mimicked the petal growth of a Chrysanthemum flower. However, the Shih Tzu was known as the "XI SHI QUAN" based on the name XI SHI, regarded as one of the most beautiful women of ancient China, and less often the Chrysanthemum Dog. These dogs grew in popularity and became officially recognized by the American Kennel Club (AKC) in 1969 under the Toy Dog category and widely recognized throughout the world, including recognition by the Federal Cynbologique International, bred in Thuin, Belgium.

DIVORCE: WHAT AN EDUCATION

One of the most recognizable individuals for the Shih Tzu breeding was Mrs. Gay Widdrington who was seen as being the person most responsible for purifying the modern Shih Tzu and breeding out the majority of known health issues which she started in 1939. Mrs. Widdrington achieved this purification by widening the pool of dogs for breeding by sourcing "pure" Shih Tzus from Europe and Norway. This greatly reduced and eliminated a large number of hereditary problems associated with these animals and is responsible for the great health of the modern Shih Tzu. However, her efforts were never recognized by the Kennel Club.

Mrs. Widdrington's work was continued by another lady: Mrs. Freda Evans in 1952. Mrs. Evans attempted to remove and correct certain features of the Shih Tzu by cross-breeding, which was highly controversial. She crossed the Shih Tzu with Pekingese dogs, which did help to improve pigmentation and create proportional facial features. Despite the controversy, these dogs were eventually widely accepted as the current "pure breed" Shih Tzu standard.

The Shih Tzu has a very long and rich history and is one of the oldest type of dogs. So, dedicated breeders were hugely responsible for the popularity and spread of the breed which enables us to have access to and enjoy this amazing animal today. The Shih Tzu history is a fascinating topic, especially to those of us that love them.

This breed of dog weighs 4 to 7.25 kilograms (8.8 to 16 pounds) with long silky hair and their name is both singular and plural. A small dog with a short muzzle, large dark eyes with a soft and long double coat. The Shih Tzu stands no more than 26.7 cm, (10.5 inches) with drop ears that are covered with long fur

THE LION DOG

and a heavily furred tail that's carried curled over the back. The coat may be of any color though a blaze of white on the forehead and tip of the tail is frequently seen. These dogs are slightly longer and ideally should carry themselves "with distinctly arrogant carriage." A very noticeable feature is the under bite, a standard requirement in this breed. The traditional long silky coat reaches to the floor and needs to be brushed daily to avoid tangles. Such brushing is important because of their long coat and fast growing hair. Often, the coat is clipped short to simplify care - a "puppy clip." P.J. was the first Shih Tzu purchased because he was a handsome little dude with the traditional colors for the breed. It was decided to just name him with initials instead of peanut butter and jelly or after myself. He was a pure breed of his kind and accredited by the American Kennel Club (AKC) which showed his name as Lucky P.J. and he was. Michiko, which means Little Lady in Japanese, was purchased six months later; I've been told that there was a princess in Japan with the same name. She was the runt of the litter that had traditional colors too; she was black and white with a face that only a mother could love. Michiko was a pure breed of her kind similar to P.J and accredited by the American Kennel Club (AKC) also which showed her name as Michiko Princess and she was too.

P.J. had been pinned by a lab twice because of the little man syndrome; he thought he was the big dog of the house. He was attacked by a mixed German Shepherd while just sitting down watching the other dogs playing. His eye was scratched by a cat because he jumped into the bushes after it. I would take him to the vet constantly because of his skin issues. One time I took him to the vet and he walked over to the scale, got weighed, and sat quietly when he got off; I looked at the girls at the office and

DIVORCE: WHAT AN EDUCATION

said, "That's not my dog." He had been bitten by a spider. Don't forget, he had three hot spots, and two abscesses. However what can I say about him, he was a friend, companion, and one loyal dog. Michiko had a problem with one of her anal glands, her eye was scratched by a pit bull, and her nose was scoped because she sniffed a twig up into her sinuses. The bacteria was eating away at her nasal bone, which cost $2500 to correct. However, Michiko was the lover of the two and I'll never find another one like her. I took her to the vet one time and the physician happened to be Asian, so when he was through with her he stated, "Dude, you have a Chinese dog with a Japanese name—that's so wrong." I told him that I didn't win naming the dog but she answered to her name well. Their marriage lasted longer than mine, my running joke, because they were together for twelve and a half years before P.J. passed; he collapsed in front of me. His behavior was nothing out of the ordinary, but I couldn't figure out what was bothering him until he died, I noticed a big clump of poop in his backside. I didn't see that because his tail was covering it. He had trouble once before moving his bowels and I helped, but it wore him out. So, I got him cleaned. Then the following day, I took him to the local vet to have an autopsy performed because I wanted to know what killed him. I was informed that he died of congestive heart failure, which supposedly runs in this breed. His mitral valve, a valve on the left side of the heart, was inflamed along with an inability to function properly. Plus, he had fluid throughout his lung fields. However, I was advised that the vet would help with his burial, so I asked, "Where do you bury dogs around here?" (which was in Blythe, California), and the reply from the vet's assistant was that "we don't bury dogs around here; we just throw them in the dumpster." I told them not to throw

THE LION DOG

my twelve-and-a-half-year-old dog in the dumpster because if that happened, I would be dumpster diving to retrieve him so I could give him the proper burial that he deserves. However, I was given a number by the vet's office to contact an individual who performs cremations and that's what I did for him. When you have two animals and one dies, you have to let the other sniff them so they know their partner is gone. I made sure that Michiko sniffed P.J. several times, because if he just disappeared, she wouldn't have known where he went. After the third time, she knew he passed.

One of the saddest things I ever saw was when Michiko sniffed a picture of P.J. that I showed to her. She would also lick his harness that I left lying around so I had to remove it. It was just heartbreaking. Michiko was well aware of P.J.'s passing and now, it was only her and she knew it. P.J. got all of the attention because he was the alpha male dog, but Michiko knew it was her time. She had a terrible cough and her oral intake was poor because she would only take three bites of her food and lie down. She barely drank from her water dish and urinary output was low or non-existent. I would come home and Michiko would lick my face briefly then stop which wasn't like her. She had been like this for three days. She would hardly walk when I took her out because she had tendonitis and arthritis after falling out of the car a few years earlier. Her eyes were covered with a blue film, but she was still able to see; I had to do something for her. So I took her to a vet in Yuma, Arizona and it was difficult because it felt that I was driving her to her death. I knew that I wasn't bringing her back home. I couldn't look at her even though she was licking my hands. The doctor, at first, thought she had emphysema; I thought she had congestive heart failure like P.J. The only way to be sure was to take an X-ray which I had done and the results weren't good. Michiko had her trachea, windpipe, curved like the letter "C" and to the right, an enlarged heart off the chest wall cavity floor pushed to the right—also with her lungs compressed full of fluid. Plus, her liver was enlarged as well. I had to put her down on the twenty third of May 2012, nearly a year after P.J.'s death. She was just two months shy of her thirteenth birthday which was the eighth of July and just like P.J., I had her cremated.

It was very quiet at my apartment after the dogs were gone and I was not greeted by them when I walked through the door. So, I had an oil painting made of each one and they are mounted on the wall. On the contrary, they are the first thing I see when I come home and enter through the door, which makes me smile.

When an animal dies that has been especially close to someone here on earth, they cross the Rainbow Bridge. There are meadows and hills for all of our special friends so they can run and play together. There is plenty of food, water, and sunshine and our friends are warm and comfortable. All the animals who were ill and old are restored to health and vigor; those who were hurt or maimed are made whole and strong again, just as we remembered them in our dreams. Also, the days and times gone by. The animals are happy and content except for one small thing; they miss that person very special to them who was left behind. They all run and play together but the day comes when one suddenly stops and looks into the distance, their bright eyes are intent and their eager bodies quiver. Suddenly, they begin to break away from the group, flying over the green grass, their legs carrying them faster and faster. You have been spotted and when you and your special friend(s) finally meet, you cling together in joyous reunion, never to be parted again. Their happy kisses rain upon your face; your hands again caress the beloved head, and you look once more into the trusting eyes of your pet(s) so long gone from your life but never absent from your heart.

Then, you cross the Rainbow Bridge together.

At 4 months "You are so cute."
At 6 months "You ate my shoes?"
At 1 year "You went potty inside again."
At 2 years "You have so much energy."
At 5 years "You're my best friend."
At 9 years "You just get me."
At 15 years "I would do that all over again if that meant bringing you back."

P.J. and Michiko had an extraordinary life; like Johnny Cash, they had been everywhere. They'd been cross country twice, up and down the state of California, spent time in Florida, Idaho, and Nevada. However, the longer we stayed in the desert I knew they wouldn't survive because they were cool weather dogs. However, they got acclimated.

They were my travel companions, after I separated from the family, because I had no one else. Over the years, I've gotten into arguments with family and friends related to the dogs because I've been told to rid myself of them and move forward. But I had them for such a long time I couldn't do that. If I put them in a kennel, P.J. would be dead in five days and Michiko, more than likely, would be adopted. So, my response would be that I would kick your ass to the curb before I got rid of my dogs.

I got them to walk and it didn't matter whether through the rain, snow, mud, and slush, because they didn't care. They enjoyed riding in the car and P.J. sat on my lap for eight years and stuck his head out the window while we were driving fast; the expression on his face was priceless.

Pets bring so much joy to their owners and increase your quality of life. Some individuals or couples decide that they don't want to have children so they purchase pets who become their kids; P.J. and Michiko were just that. There are so many wonderful moments with them that are too numerous to mention, but I will touch on a few of them that will make you smile.

When we were no longer a part of the family unit, we resided in Mountain View, California (2003), which has been stated. I started to walk the dogs, got them accustomed to riding in the car and going to parks. They would walk three to four times a day so we didn't go to the same place; we'd visit several parks during the day. They would walk side by side and when one stopped to sniff something or take care of business, the other would wait. They wouldn't venture far. When I fell while we were walking; they'd turn around and walk over to see what happened? I didn't realize how intelligent the Shih Tzu was until I took them for a walk in Orlando, Florida (2003) after being summoned by my mother. It was dark and I knew the number on the apartment building. We were out walking for two and a half hours zigging and zagging in this complex. However, P.J. led us straight back to the front door. One day while in Vero Beach, Florida (2004) where we moved closer to my parents, the dogs jumped out of the car and disappeared. I went searching for them and even listened to the barking in the neighborhood to see if I could find them; it had been thirty minutes with no success. So, I headed back to the dollhouse, where we were living in the woods, and found them sitting outside the front door.

THE LION DOG

During our travels, we met so many people and different breeds of dogs. For example, there was a Saint Bernard pup who got down on the level of P.J. and Michiko. Other breeds were an Akita, Basset Hound, Bichon, Boston Terrier, Cavalier King Charles Spaniel, Chihuahua, Collie, Dachshund, Doberman Pinscher, German Shepherd, Jack Russell Terrier, Japanese Chin, Labrador Retriever, Lhasa Apso, Miniature Pinscher, Poodles, Miniature Schnauzer, Papillion, Pekingese, Pomeranian, Pug, Siberian Husky, and Yorkshire Terrier.

Eventually, I had to return to California (2005) in an attempt to resolve my legal issues and I took the dogs along. When we took a break after driving for several hours, they enjoyed using the elevator at every hotel or motel and they circled the facility several times, walking inside, outside, and around it. Many individuals that I met while with the dogs wanted to take Michiko home, but I would state that they were a pair and that if you took one, you took them both. I couldn't split them up because they had been together for so many years. As I said, their marriage lasted longer than mine. They were so funny at times because they would sit at the entrance to an outside bar with live music and greet everyone who was coming there to enjoy the evening (at the marina in Chula Vista, California, 2006 -2009). Chula Vista was just outside of Imperial Beach where we were residing. Sometimes, the waitress would bring out scraps of meat and water for them, plus they were starting to get well known because they would always walk to that area when we went to the marina. Michiko would tease P.J. because she would be given a milk bone cookie and it would remain in front of her; P.J. would bark at her because he wanted it after finishing his. Every time P.J. tried to get the cookie she'd left on the floor, Michiko would pounce on it before he

DIVORCE: WHAT AN EDUCATION

could obtain it. Another time, for no reason Michiko would start to bite P.J.'s feet while he was lying down so Michiko would be asking for it. I would say, "Go get her boy" to P.J but he would pause then I would repeat it again and he was off. They would chase each other around the apartments in which we'd taken up residence and you would hear doink as one of them hit their head on the coffee table. Then, Michiko would jump onto the sofa and P.J. would bark at her because he couldn't get her. Eventually, he would and I would have to pull him off of her.

Shih Tzus like to have contact with their owners; they lie beside you if you're on the floor, sofa, or bed. They just want to have that human contact. Even in bed, they will position themselves to the point that you are unable to move because they've tucked you in so tight.

I would be greeted at the door by them, which I miss the most, as they would show their unconditional love licking my face for twenty minutes.

P.J. and Michiko had an extraordinary life, as I said, because they've been at my side through it all; the ups and downs, the good times and bad. But I made sure they were loved and I received that in return. Also, they had a stable environment everywhere we went during my career. They were such wonderful companions and such an important part of my life; I could talk about them for hours. One day, I plan to purchase another pair of Shih Tzus but until then, I know that they are waiting until we are reunited again. It will be a joyous occasion as we cross the Rainbow Bridge together.

Chapter 9
MATERIALISTIC WORLD

It's been costly over the years because I've lost so much that I don't know where to start.

First of all, you should never let a woman handle the finances during a marriage or you should have separate accounts and I'll tell you why. The first thing I lost was the 1997 Jeep Wrangler; it was repossessed in 2001 because payments were not met or paid at all. The one thing that's irreplaceable was my military mementos and memories that I had at a storage facility in Melbourne, Florida. My ex-wife had no regard for any personal items of mine and all of it was sold. I might be able to retrieve the thirtieth anniversary of the ship - the USS Saratoga CV 60- a cruise book which was made while being overseas and serving on the vessel. However, I would have to pay nearly $300 for it when I initially acquired it for free. The photos, stories, cartoon drawings, jackets and anything else I'd obtained while in the service and the countries I had the opportunity to visit are all gone. There were moments and events captured in print, for example, I had pictures of two Libyan gunboats that were covered with smoke because

DIVORCE: WHAT AN EDUCATION

they were on fire in the water. Also, there was a naval hat that I purchased on the ship during the time I served in the military. I had it for twenty-five years until it fell apart; I made another one but it took several pieces to put together. However, it's not the same; even though it looks like the original, it wasn't bought on the vessel. A cartoon strip drawn by a crew member describing and illustrating the life and times while living onboard an aircraft carrier; it was well done and very funny.

Most of the items that I had to relinquish were personal; even though some of them could be retrieved, others were not or couldn't be because of the inability to afford them. During the marriage, we were able to secure a time share in Puerto Vallarta, Mexico for $1400, with our joint account and payments were made from this account by her signature. However, both our names were on the checks, but the court didn't view it that way. My ex-wife claimed that she made all of the payments toward this item for the upkeep and maintenance so we could have access to it in the second week of March each year. We both made payments toward the time share but at the settlement conference in 2005, I was overruled by the judicial system because I didn't have any documentation to show the court that I had made payments. So, it was lost because the court awarded it to her. After I lost the Jeep Wrangler in 2001; I tried to purchase another vehicle so I could continue working and support the family, but my ex-wife was furious. It was a 1980 Chevy Citation that had an eight track player. The eight track tape recording system was popular from 1965 to the late 1970s while today, it has become an icon of obsolescence. It was a great commercial success and paved the way for all sorts of innovations in portable listening. The eight track tape consisted of an endless loop of standard one fourth inch magnetic tape, housed in a plastic cartridge. On the tape were eight parallel soundtracks corresponding to four stereo programs. For many people old enough to have owned an eight track system, it is a technology associated with the automobile and in-car listening. Ironically, however, it was first developed not by the auto industry, but by a leading aircraft manufacturer, Learjet Corporation. The eight track player still functioned, the vehicle was in excellent condition and had only one owner. The car would cost $1850 but my ex-wife argued over purchasing it; I needed a vehicle. Every time that I wanted to make a payment toward the Jeep Wrangler, she would state, "That could wait." Well, she waited too long and it was lost.

When I was summoned by my mother to return home to Florida in 2003; I took the 1998 Dodge Durango we obtained. While addressing family issues related to my father, I was notified by Wells Fargo Financial Acceptance Corporation that the vehicle needed to be surrendered for non-payment. The reason for non-payment was because Geico Insurance Company increased the insurance rates on the automobile. At that time, I was unable to afford the Dodge Durango because maintaining this item would cost over $1000. I'd just secured a place of residence six months after returning home to Florida that I needed to get settled with the dogs and this took precedence over the vehicle. However, I was able to purchase another means of transportation; it was a 2004 Nissan Sentra from Wallace Nissan of Stuart, Florida. I could afford the payments and insurance, along with my place of residence. I had explained the situation with my ex-wife to the representative at the dealership and he advised me to have the Dodge Durango repossessed. I had informed my first attorney before he quit the case, and he told me to retain the car and not have this done. My ex-wife wanted to take responsibility for the vehicle and I was willing to place it on a flatbed truck so it could be shipped to her front door in California, send $500, and get her attorney off my back. She would have to renew the registration, get insurance and new license plate tags. I had several conversations with her concerning the Dodge Durango but they turned into arguments and I was threatened by her with jail time. I then called Deanna, a Wells Fargo financial acceptance representative, and made her aware what transpired in the conversations with my ex-wife which were recorded and transcribed into their computer. I had the Dodge Durango longer than expected and was waiting to hear from her and know her course of action for this car. She responded on the 16th of April 2004 and said, "I wasn't going to do anything until the 13th of May." So when I was able to reach her again, she stated, "I can't make a payment on the vehicle because I'm unemployed (which she made no effort to obtain), and I can't afford it." Wells Fargo Financial Corporation was made aware again, along with the threats of jail. Since neither of us could manage the vehicle, I had to surrender it.

According to the court, since I had exclusive and temporary use of the vehicle and had it repossessed, I was responsible to pay the difference if the car was sold for a lesser amount. However, the court documentation read that I had exclusive and temporary use of the vehicle that we own; it doesn't say I. I still have the contract with her signature on it, making her just as responsible regardless. The difference was $9000 after it was sold and this amount has been increasing over the years; I refuse to pay the entire balance on the car when she should be held accountable for it as well. During the settlement conference in 2005, she wanted to be reimbursed for five payments she made on the vehicle and one payment was made after it was handed over to Wells Fargo. I tried to get two of my attorneys to subpoena these records to show the court the dealings of this woman, but that never happened. How could an individual request reimbursement for payments made on community property when she stated a year earlier that she couldn't afford it nor could she even make a payment. I tried to stress this to my attorneys, but they just ignored me.

Child support had taken nearly my entire check so I was unable to remain at my place of residence, which was a doll house in Vero Beach, Florida. I had to reside with my parents again. My mother understood that I needed to return to California so I could put this legal matter to rest; I told her "if I leave, Dad will die." Sure enough he did pass away one day after Father's Day 2005, and I've never forgiven my ex-wife for that. My father wasn't a material thing, but it falls under the category of a loss. After he died, I have received a visit from him three times: the first, was during a dream to let me know he was in a good place: the second, we were sitting around the kitchen table and I received a pamphlet from him to quit smoking; finally, his spirit appeared while I was driving. When I was driving, I had a strong sense of beer and was in an area that didn't produce it. My father was a big beer drinker, but not an alcoholic; so when I called him three times, the scent went away. So, it's like the song by David Ball, a country singer, called "Riding with Private Malone." It talks about how while driving he gets the feeling that if he turned real quick he'd see a soldier riding shotgun in the seat right next to him. I knew that day my father was by my side in the car.

Speaking of fathers, my ex-wife was arrested for assault with a deadly weapon and disturbing the peace in 2001 at her sister's house in Reno, Nevada while watching a video of their deceased father.

DIVORCE: WHAT AN EDUCATION

My mother sold her villa to help pay for my first hip replacement in 2006. I secured a position briefly in Santa Ana, California. Then I accepted a position with the State of California, working within the prison system. I had to find a place to call home because I was living in a hotel room with the dogs. I located a duplex in a small town outside San Diego, California called Imperial Beach but didn't realize it had no air conditioning. However, it was only ten blocks from the beach. So, I slowly began to get settled. I was evicted from there in 2009 by child support because they seized my income tax return and I was thrown out on the street by them. Unfortunately I was unable to take any of the furnishings that I had purchased. I had a small sectional, queen size bed, and a coffee table that cost over $1000 which I had to leave behind. A portable air conditioner from Sears that cost $500 and an air conditioner I placed in the kitchen door that led to the backyard which was $96. Two fans and an entertainment center to support the television was valued at $50. I could only take items that would fit within the 2007 Ford Explorer that I had, along with the dogs. I didn't have a trailer or a hitch for the vehicle and couldn't afford it because I was broke and now homeless.

I became unemployed in 2010 after working two positions as a travel nurse. So, I traveled to the Northwest where I had four possible permanent jobs, but they all fell through. I drove from the Northwest to Las Vegas for a job interview but I didn't get the position so I started to call nursing agencies to secure employment. While sleeping in the car with my dogs one night in Las Vegas, the police noticed my California license plates were expired so they physically removed them from my vehicle. I tried to register the vehicle in Nevada and went to the Department of Motor Vehicles (DMV) three times, stood in long lines while the dogs sat in the car under a shade tree. On my third attempt, I was able to achieve a temporary permit. Finally, I was able to secure employment in Antioch, California; however, I was presented with an opportunity to work at a small hospital in Blythe, California that was paying well so I could correct my financial problems. I had to make a decision; driving eight hours on a major freeway without any insurance or license plates on the car, get pulled over by the police and have everything I own including my animals taken away. Or, I could drive three hours on a backroad without getting pulled over and make it to my destination. So, I headed south from Las Vegas to the desert in Blythe.

While I was working at Palo Verde Hospital in Blythe, California, I noticed that my vehicle wasn't parked at my place of residence which was just across the street from the facility. Chase Auto Finance repossessed it. I was able to make a few insurance payments while I was unemployed, but no car payments. According to Chase Auto Finance, I owed $1200 and was informed by the towing company that they could take the vehicle with the assistance of the police without notification to the owner. The towing company stated, "The plan was to transport the car to Lake Havasu, Arizona for it to be sold." I couldn't allow that to happen because I already had two vehicles repossessed and I wasn't about to have a third. So, I hustled and was able to pay half of the $1200 and petitioned my mother for the other half to reclaim it and repay her. It was exhilarating to drive my car off the impound lot, but I was advised by Chase Auto Finance that if I missed one payment on the car, it would be taken without any questions and I wouldn't be able to regain it again. On the contrary, I have one more payment and it's mine. It's like the country song by Clint Black, "One More Payment" It goes a little like

DIVORCE: WHAT AN EDUCATION

this: I've been footin' the bill for some time step by step and line by dotted line. Well, I haven't bought the farm yet but I'm not that far behind; I've got one more payment and it's mine. I was able to achieve this, so I don't have any more payments toward it.

I've lost hundreds and thousands of dollars trying to put this legal matter to rest; I've leaned on my family, especially my mother, friends and coworkers and I can't say enough about them. A lot of time, energy, and effort has been spent over a six-year period to solve this issue. I spent countless hours, days, and months preparing and submitting court documentation along with appeals during that time. These matters have been expensive. One year alone, I spent $1300 on air fare, not including car rentals that total over $500. Plus, lodging cost $682. I spent $110 in gas and parking, $100 in food, and over $300 withdrawn from ATMs. Seventy-five dollars of court documentation copies and $730 in appeals. There were times that were so unbearable that I would break down and cry because it was just awful. After eleven years, I finally found some stability in my life. I'm reminded of the quote from the movie, "The Patriot" which starred Mel Gibson. The Patriot is a fictional 2000 American historical war film that takes place in rural York County, South Carolina and depicts the story of an American swept into the American Revolutionary War when his family is threatened. Benjamin Martin is a composite figure who the scriptwriter claims is based on four real American Revolutionary War heroes: Andrew Pickens, Francis Marion, Daniel Morgan and Thomas Sumter. In the movie, it was always preached to stay the course. As my father would say, "When you're driving and it's raining, you just keep going because you'll drive out of it eventually," which I have.

Chapter 10
FORWARD

During the movie, "City Slickers," a 1991 American Western comedy film, Billy Crystal's character (Mitch) looks to Phil, played by Daniel Stern, because he's so upset he screwed up his life and starts to cry. His buddies, including Bruno Kirby as Ed, reminded Phil when they were kids playing baseball, and couldn't agree on a play or call; they would yell 'do over.'

I recall that scene because it had so much meaning. When I was a child, I would do the same thing. They continued with the analogy and explained to Phil that his life was a do over, and I agree.

I left the family unit at the beginning of January 2003 as I stated and started on a new adventure to redo my life over or at least get a better perspective and have a sense of order. This endeavor would take the better part of eleven years just to get my finances under control.

It began when I left with the dogs, who became my traveling companions, and the 1998 Dodge Durango that was purchased during the marriage. However, my ex-wife held the vehicle hostage for two days before the journey began. I called Wells Fargo Bank in an attempt to remove her name from financial responsibly because she didn't want to be held liable if the vehicle was repossessed; I was advised that it couldn't be accomplished. So, I was granted the vehicle from her and departed. You need to be careful what you purchase as a couple during a marriage because it will become community property if you decide to end it.

It was difficult at first because I was residing at a motel with my animals while working for a hospital in Fremont, California. It was small; however, the night clerk would take the dogs down to the lobby and watch over them as customers registered into the facility. The days that I didn't work, I was constantly looking for a place of residence that was better suited for myself and the dogs. I found an apartment in Mountain View, California, on top of a garage that had a seventeen by forty backyard along with a terrace and a basketball hoop, which the dogs just loved. With every apartment, utilities and furnishings needed to be handled, then groceries. However, the dogs were kept warm in their house coats, along with a heater I bought until I could get the electric established; they didn't mind because they were cool weather animals. The first week of February 2003, the telephone continued to ring; it was my ex-wife who started to call for money while crying over the phone because the rent wasn't paid and she was afraid of being evicted. She wanted to know who was going to take care of these babies, meaning the children. It wasn't my problem because she was the one that ended the marriage. Eighty five percent of divorces are filed by women because they know the laws favor them according to *No BS Divorce Strategies for Men*. I was attempting to start fresh in life and she needed to figure out how to resolve the issue.

FORWARD

I suggested that she advise our landlord, Tony, and explain the situation, but she expected that I should handle it. She continually tried to use reverse psychology, stating "they're your babies too." However when there was a crisis, they were my children. On the contrary, when she was mad at me, they were her children. She tried to have it both ways and, apparently, she believed that she could. Because of her actions and her perception that I wasn't concerned or interested in helping, her reply was, "I see how you are." I was dealing with everyday life after being released from the family unit— such as working, caring for the dogs, and dealing with my finances. But I was able to release the security deposit from our previous address so she could find a place that was affordable for her and the children. As the phone continued to ring, I was informed by her of items that were ignored. For example, the 1998 Dodge Durango hadn't been paid for. And, every time I had a conversation with her, she still hadn't gained any employment to support the children. Also, she wasn't receiving any assistance from her mother because her mother knew of her actions and knew her actions were wrong. She had no source of income and failed an exam at school; I told her I was sorry, but her reply was sarcastic -"No you're not." I mentioned to her that I didn't know what she was doing or what type of game she was playing and I didn't know why. She called one night because she had a pharmacological test for school and wondered if I would help because she was terrible at math, so I spent two hours on the phone with her so she could understand it. This was an effort to see her succeed; then we could both move forward with our lives. Later, I learned that she was successful; I helped her get into the nursing program and never wanted to see her fail.

I was constantly harassed from this woman about money for

months; she would call two to three times a week requesting it. So, I decided to provide her with $2000 a month in an effort to separate myself from her and the children. However, I was only making $1200 dollars a month and it was a struggle to maintain activities of daily living. My ex-wife made a statement that she would quit the nursing program to support the kids, but she never secured active employment and had no intention of doing that, even though I had several conversations with her on how to get a job and where to go and obtain one. But she made no effort to secure one. At one time, she was working on securing a position and even applied for three through the newspaper; however, because of school, she turned down a position after receiving a return call. She could have landed a job and worked out a schedule where she could go to school to benefit herself and the company that offered her the opportunity to work. In her eyes, I was expected to continue managing her expenses and needs when she made no effort to help herself; remember, I was released from the family unit by her. She was denied financial assistance because I made too much money, but she had no one to blame but herself. I suggested that her sister get another job because it's not like she hasn't worked two jobs before; also, the eldest child would be working soon and could contribute to the household. When I was older, living with my parents, I would contribute to the household while I was working. However with the support of a classmate, who was her new lover, my ex wife ignored all of my suggestions. She had secured a new residence with him, his autistic child, the children, and her sister. But she didn't pay the utility bills from the previous address prior to moving, and I had to cover it because it was in my name. She had no intention of settling this debt.

FORWARD

I had been summoned by my mother while I continued to reside in Mountain View, California; I was advised that my father had become ill and I needed to return to Florida.

I wrote a letter to my ex-wife explaining my situation and the fact that I wouldn't be able to support her and the children because all of my time, money, and effort would be devoted to him. My father's prognosis wasn't good; he would probably live another three to eight years more or less. It had been two and a half years and for the first time my mother needed my help. I thought my ex-wife would understand, considering that her father had passed away years ago, but I was mistaken.

I sent her a letter in May 2003, to inform her that as of the first of September I could no longer support her. I was willing to assist the children voluntarily. I felt as though she had abused the privilege. So I was going to cut her down to $300 a week and as September was nearing, I would cut her down to $250. Finally, I would stop altogether at the end of August because three months should have been enough time for her to find a job. She was advised not to call, leave messages on my answering machine or cell phone because I wouldn't respond to them. Also, she was told not to have the kids call and try to get information to benefit her. For example, I received a phone call from the eldest child upon my return to Florida, my ex-wife had her state, "I want to send you something," so I gave her my address. A few days later, I was served with divorce papers. I had withdrawn from our joint account three times and she requested I cease doing that, upon which I agreed. However, I was living in tremendous pain with my hips (that eventually needed to be replaced) and it was difficult to walk from one bank to the other so I could deposit money in our account. One day, I had to physically enter the bank to make a deposit to the joint account because she had frozen my ATM card after I told her that I wouldn't use it. She had never mentioned doing it. The type of behavior she would exhibit; she would say or do one thing and if you were not looking, you would get stabbed in the back.

I was advised that she reactivated our cell phones except mine so I had to buy a new one. The house phone was turned off before I had the opportunity to terminate the services; it remained current so she could inquire about other houses to rent. I received a statement from her regarding the computer, which was $208.76, which I paid. I got a request from her to have the Franchise State Tax Board withdraw money out of my account instead of our joint one for the amount we owed for the year 2001, which I did. I closed the account with the cable company because I received a bill with my name on it as the primary person responsible when she promised to place the service in her name. I think she did this for spite. A collection agency had reached out because of a video game that was returned late in February, when I wasn't even there. It just shows such a lack of responsibility from her and the children but it was handled. I was living on $200 a month after depositing money in our account and paying off a few bills; I was broke most of the time and could only purchase one thing for the week or not.

I needed to start taking care of myself and detach myself from her and move forward. I did everything within my ability to close accounts, pay off debts, dissociate my name from hers, and make preparations to return home to help my parents.

My parents were the most important people during this period. Unfortunately, my father has been gone for nearly a decade now. When I took him for testing at the University of San

FORWARD

Francisco in 2003 for Frontal Temporal Dementia/Progressive Aphasia, I had to remove his necklace. I didn't know what to do with it so I wore it; however, I'm not an individual that wears jewelry. After his death in 2005, I requested that item from my mother and on the days that I don't have to work, I wear the necklace that belonged to him so he's always close to my heart and never forgotten.

Chapter 11
FATHERS' RIGHTS

The modern fathers' rights movement in the U.S. emerged with the founding of Divorce Racket Busters in California in 1960 to protest California's divorce laws which they claimed discriminated against men in alimony, child support settlements and in a presumption of maternal custody. The group expanded into other states, changing its name to Divorce Reform in 1961. With the increase in divorce rates in the 1960s and 1970s, more local grassroots men's organizations grew up devoted to divorce reform and by the 1980s, there were a total of more than two hundred fathers' rights groups active in almost every state.

These groups focused their actions on what they viewed as gender discrimination in family law by engaging in political activities such as lobbying state legislatures, filing class action suits, picketing courthouses, and monitoring judges' decision through court watches. With the 1990s came the emergence of new and larger organizations such as National Fatherhood Initiative and the American Fathers Coalition.

Several unsuccessful efforts were made to found a national

organization. As a result, the movement remains mainly a loose coalition of local groups.

Members of the fathers' movement assert that fathers are discriminated against as a result of gender bias in family law and custody decisions have been a denial of equal rights and that the influence of money has corrupted family law. The movement's primary focus has been to campaign (including lobbying and research) for formal legal rights for fathers, sometimes for the children, changes to family law related to child custody, support and maintenance. Also, domestic violence and the family court system as a whole needed to be monitored. Fathers' rights groups provide emotional and practical support for members during separation and divorce.

There are many groups that advocate for fathers' rights in the United States and elsewhere. Each group promotes father's rights in the family law system, works to change laws to discriminate less against fathers, and advocates for shared parenting and joint custody in cases where fathers are separated from their children.

Fathers and Families is an advocacy group fighting for fathers' rights, shared custody and family court reform in the United States. They have advocated for and helped pass legislation in several states, reforming family court law, child support, and custody to reduce the discrimination against fathers. They've placed a shared custody amendment on the ballot in Massachusetts and advocated for its eventual passage. Also, they've helped pass bills in California, Arizona, and Indiana to protect disabled parents from family court financial abuses. They helped pass paternity fraud legislation in California and spearheaded a massive nationwide grassroots protest campaign against anti-father PBS show on child custody, successfully forcing production of an even-handed documentary.

DIVORCE: WHAT AN EDUCATION

DADS America is a nations fathers' rights organization that works to help educate fathers on their rights and strategies for shared custody and empowers them to use that knowledge to strengthen relationships with children through father-involved custody. DADS America has prepared a Fathers' Bill of Rights that defines what fathers can and can't do under the law and calls for reforms to eliminate discrimination against them. They have local chapters in nine states (Alabama, Alaska, Delaware, Missouri, New Jersey, New York, Oregon, Washington, and Canada) working within their own jurisdictions to make changes. Also, they summarize news articles, court cases and other resources about their rights and responsibilities in the family legal system. Sample legal documentation, including a model prenuptial agreement, are offered on their website; members have access to a chat room and legal assistance.

Dad's Divorce is a website dedicated to educating fathers on the issues of divorce, child custody, and child support.

Fathers for Equal Rights vision is that society will recognize the right of every child to have a healthy relationship with both parents, regardless of the status of their family structure. Fathers for Equal Rights operates the National Fathers' Center which has a host of information for fathers about their rights and legislative advocacy. Fathers can find legal counsel, learn about fathers' rights efforts around the country, and get tips for dealing with the family court system and more.

Many would argue that there is gender bias in the family court. Some would say that the court favors women while others claim that the court has a bias toward men. Each side sees bias; in fact, the court used to routinely award custody to the mother, assuming that she was the more nurturing parent. Some states, like

FATHERS' RIGHTS

California, assume that each parent has equal rights and responsibilities regarding a child but many feel, like myself, that fathers' rights are systematically ignored in favor of the mother. At least it was true during my case.

The role of the father is often discounted or seen as less important than that of the mother but studies show that children do better in school, relationships, and home life when both parents are involved in the lives of their children. Sociologist Dr. David Popenoe, a pioneer in fatherhood, stated, "Fathers are far more than just a second adult in the home. Involved fathers bring positive benefits to their children that no other person is as likely to bring. Because of the importance of this role, fathers' equal rights are essential." Several studies showed that with fathers involved and nurturing, young children have better cognitive abilities, linguistic capabilities, and higher IQs.

During a divorce, fathers have the right to be involved in their children's lives, interacting and spending time with them. They have equal say in important decisions regarding them, the right to participate in parenting, seeing school and medical records. Also, they have the right to help decide which doctors and dentists they see and the right to participate in medical treatment decisions, disciplining, with no interference from the other parent. These rights don't require a court order to obtain; however, a fathers' rights attorney can help ensure that your rights are upheld and that your case is effectively presented to the court. So if there is a bias against you, the attorney can help tip the scales in your favor or at least balance the scales (I don't know if I believe that). In California, men enjoy the same rights as women and are entitled to equal custody and support that was non-existent in regard to my legal matter.

DIVORCE: WHAT AN EDUCATION

The days of stay-at-home moms that got custody of the children are long gone. Fathers have and deserve the same rights as mothers do when it comes to caring for a child. In today's modern world, both parents often work to support their families and in some instances, the stay-at-home parent is the father not the mother; unfortunately, the laws have not been able to keep up with the times and the significant change in typical family dynamics. A father does matter in the lives of his children because study after study shows that there exists a variety of negative effects on children that don't have a father in their lives. Children without a father are more likely to use illegal drugs, drop out of school, and likely to commit domestic violence (for example, my daughter). The majority of teenage murderers come from fatherless families. Without a strong father relationship in a child's life, a child has little chance to succeed and become a productive member of society. A father's knowledge of what pitfalls are present in a case of fathers' fights and custody is imperative to setting the stage for success and nothing is more worth fighting for.

Common mistakes fathers make are moving out of the home where the child lives, having a messy home or studio apartment, not having a steady job, and not fighting against trumped up 'order of protection' charges originated by the mother.

Contrary to popular belief about fathers' rights, child visitation rights are not automatically your rights at all. They are considered the rights of the child. The terms of visitation are something that you have to account for in a parenting plan, or fight for in family court if you are denied access to your children as their father. Neither parent has the right to see his nor her children if it is deemed not in the children's best interest. During a divorce or separation the court makes decisions regarding child custody, child support, and visitation rights in the best interest of the child. But, the court didn't want to hear any of the circumstances in my case.

Once I subscribed to a Fathers' Rights organization and reviewed the material, there wasn't much to offer, but there were some helpful tips. The Parents' Golden Rule states that there's always three sides to the story: he said, she said, and the truth. However, the court doesn't search for that. The five biggest mistakes made in court. You fail to respond and your ex wife will get everything in her petition and more. You listen to incorrect legal advice as I have with two of three attorneys. You sign bad settlement agreements such as a Stipulated Judgment or Marital Settlement Agreement and never sign an agreement if it's not what you want, you don't like it, or you can't perform it. You become frustrated and give up because the court gave your ex-wife everything and you feel that you were the victim. Finally, you never want to see what the judge might say. During the legal procedures, you should have an established residence for six months and you can file for divorce after three months, but remember that you need to respond within ten to thirty days of any court documentation you receive. The dissolution of marriage is quick and easy, but it's useless filing. However, you can petition for an annulment of the marriage such as to void it—meaning, the marriage was unlawful before occurrence based upon incestuous, marriage between relatives or bigamous (one party already married). Fraud is very difficult to prove in court and you need to show intent to commit fraud.

- Forced marriage from duress or threat of harm.
- Physical incapacity is the inability of one party to function

sexually; my ex-wife just stopped having sex and I was advised that she hadn't been able to get pregnant for seven years.
- If both parties are unable to divide the community property, the court should divide the assets 50/50, but I wasn't granted any of that from my marriage.

If I wanted to terminate or modify the spousal support, it would be based on my employment and income; however, my ex-wife refused to obtain any gainful employment during these proceedings. Since I don't receive my tax and state returns or any tax breaks, I learned that you file exempt on your W-4 form. There are two things in life that are certain: death and taxes; so I'd rather pay the Internal Revenue Service a little more money at the end the year than someone who doesn't deserve it.

Chapter 12
SYNOPSIS

You'll never know the character, strength, or perseverance of individuals unless you walk a mile in their shoes and that's what I've done. I wanted you to lace up my boots and walk through my neighborhood, (meaning this book), see what I've been through—my experiences and obstacles I had to overcome in an attempt to regain my life. I feel as though I'm the Buck Weaver of family law. Buck Weaver played third base for the Chicago White Sox during the 1919 World Series against the Cincinnati Reds, better known as the Black Sox Scandal. After being banned from baseball, he spent the rest of his life trying to clear his name.

Alec Baldwin made a few key points in his book, *"A Promise to Ourselves" A Journey through Fatherhood and Divorce* which I would like to reiterate.

First, you want to get a prenup. I'm not a celebrity but I think it's a way of protecting yourself and your assets.

Second, you want to file first, which has some advantages that I didn't know. If you file first, you are setting the tone. However if you are named the defendant in a court proceeding, it leaves you counter-punching much of the time, which I've been doing for years.

Third, you should never hire an attorney by word of mouth. He/she might have been successful with other cases, but it doesn't mean he/she will do the same for you, which I learned the hard way.

Fourth, you want to make sure your attorney explains in detail what lies ahead. I would agree with this because he/she should outline their strategy and how it will get accomplished.

Five, you should try mediation if your spouse is willing to compromise. Mediation could continue for more than six months before you should consider going to court; however, you should have interim custody orders in place within ninety days after separation.

Six, you should demand in mediation (petition for in court) that you and your ex attend a minimum of twelve sessions of divorce co-parenting if you believe that alienation is a factor in your case. I should have done this for the girls because I was kept away from them by their mother. Their mother refused to assist with transportation or financially so I could be with them. It doesn't help your position if you're not spending time with the children. Seven, you shouldn't hide your assets because you will be penalized by the court.

Eight, you might want to set up a few sessions with a therapist who works in family law. You don't want a court-appointed evaluator to coach you; you simply want that person to explain the process and what evaluators look for in such sessions if you plan to fight for custody of the children. Do not rely on your attorney to help you.

Nine, you might want to find a therapist that you can trust

SYNOPSIS

who will guide you through the changes and decisions that you will certainly encounter.

Ten, you don't want to make your home a shrine to your child(ren). I have several photographs of the children and carry a picture of each one; I always thought about them over the years and how their lives were until we were able to reconnect.

Eleven, you should put you and your ex's drug and alcohol issues on the table. I don't have any drug issues because I don't do them and I quit drinking alcohol years ago; however, I did enter into the court my ex wife's assault with a deadly weapon and disturbing the peace.

Twelve, you should ask for orders, in court or in mediation, that provide for some flexibility of schedule, particularly in terms of your work and career. I would recommend this because when I couldn't return the youngest child on time related to my work, it appeared in the court documentation and was used against me.

It has been brought to my attention that I'm bashing women when I start to discuss my marital issues, and the opinion of people might not change after reading this material. This is far from the truth; I'm just very cautious when it comes to the opposite sex. I'm reminded of the quote from Roy Schneider, who portrayed Chief Brody, from the second movie of "Jaws": "I'm not about to go through that hell again," (referring to the discovery of a second shark which he explains to the town council of Amityville). It's how I feel about being married again because it's going to take someone really special before I utter the words, "I do."

In society, many individuals do not believe in marriage vows as most did many years ago. As a child, I viewed marriage as being permanent because my parents were married for forty-five years, until the death of my father. They had their faults but remained

DIVORCE: WHAT AN EDUCATION

with each other through the ups and downs, the good and bad, and death, as the marriage vows stated. I believe that a relationship has to have the following: trust (because without it, there wouldn't be a relationship or marriage), open honest communication, and a healthy sex life. I feel that a relationship or marriage is like a piece of clay that you continually need to work at.

Since being released from the family unit, I couldn't say that I came out smelling like a rose; however, Tim Robbins character, Andy Dufresne in the movie "The Shawshank Redemption," crawled to his freedom through five hundred yards of foul smelling shit which is the length of five football fields that no one could imagine. I may never be free from this but I was able to pick up the shattered pieces of my life and move forward. Fifteen years ago, I placed negativity on the shelf because I don't have time for that or individuals that are egotistical, self-centered, or what-have-you-done-for-me-lately, regardless of family or friend. I've surrounded myself with positive people and look for that quality in everything that I encounter these days. I don't have time for drama or bullshit that occurs in everyday life because it's too short. So I guess you're wondering why I put my thoughts and experiences on paper. It's because I wanted to inform and educate individuals, particularly men, before they venture down the path of divorce. They need to be aware—have the knowledge about the dos and don'ts of family law/divorce, and what could happen if they choose this route, so mistakes like mine aren't made. There have been many, such as signing court documentation agreements that weren't in my best interest after voicing my concerns. My legal representatives, at least two of them, weren't proficient enough to handle my case. I was angry because of what my ex-wife had done but placing my anger, hostility, and profanity in

SYNOPSIS

written form then sending to someone was a bad idea because you can never take that back. However, document, document, document everything that occurs because documentation will be essential for you. Be aware of child support, they will freeze your assets without you knowing if you have a child support order for the children that you had during the marriage. After reading the material that I've presented, some people, particularly women, may still think that I'm bashing them, but it's amazing how one person, who happens to be a woman, has had such a negative impact on her family, like myself and her children. With sperm banks, invitro fertilization, and artificial insemination, women don't need a man to have a child; however, there are some that will entrap men so they have to support her for the rest of her life. On the contrary, there are men who are deadbeat fathers, but I wasn't one of them. There are men who are Baby Daddy's but are not a part of the family unit or the children's lives. There are men who've stepped up and been a man to a single mother and her children, but they're never commended for doing such; I was one of those men. However, my efforts weren't good enough and every person that has heard this story has stated, as I've said before, "This is Wrong."

CREDITS

There are many people that I need to acknowledge because without them I wouldn't have survived.

My father always stated, "If you have five good friends that you can count on your hand that will be there with no questions asked, you were fortunate." As the saying goes, "Behind every great man, there lies a woman" which is true.

First and foremost, Dolores Vessey, my mother, has been a rock; I owe her more than I could ever imagine. She has been at my side the entire time during this ordeal and there's nothing that I wouldn't do for her.

My cousin, Chris Farland, and my friend, Chris Long, who were there in my time of need when I was homeless for a month living out of hotel rooms and my car with the dogs.

Dr. Jim Wichser, who I considered a father figure because mine had passed away; he would provide wisdom and guidance when needed.

Eunice Deleon, a dear and true friend that provided an insight from a woman's perspective when I needed it—an individual that always had an empathetic ear and would listen to my concerns.

Rebecca Jones, who's the CEO of her own travel company

CREDITS

for nurses: Sharps Medical Solution. I was able to secure employment in Las Vegas with her assistance because I was about to lose everything and be back on the street again.

Paul Simone and his wife, Pearl, who opened up their home while I was on assignment in Las Vegas after getting back to the mainland from Hawaii with their financial help.

BIBLIOGRAPHY

1. History of Divorce in America- Suite 101.com -Clark, Charles S. "Is It Time to Crack Down on Easy Divorces?" CQ Researcher. 409-432. May 10, 1996
    a. Jost, Kenneth and Robinson, Marilyn "What Can Be Done to Help Children of Divorce?" Children and Divorce. CQ Researcher. Volume One June 7, 1991
    b. May, Elaine Tyler. Copyright Cathy Herold - Cathy Herold lives in southern California. She has a BA in English and minor in African American Studies from UCLA and a master' degree.
    c. "The Pressure to Provide: Class, Consumerism, and Divorce in Urban America, 1880-1920." Journal of Social History. Winter 1978, Volume 12 Issue 2.
2. The Evolution of Divorce > Publications > National Affairs -www.nationalaffairs.com/publications/detail/the- evolution - of - divorce
3. History of Divorce in the US -www.articledashboard.com/Article/The-History-of-Divorce-In-The-US/971637
4. Divorce and Custody - The Colonial Era and Early Repub-

BIBLIOGRAPHY

lic, the Nineteenth Century -www.faqs.org/childhood/Co-Fa/Divorce-and Custody.html

5. Divorce in the United States - Wikipedia, the free encyclopedia -en.wikipedia.org/wiki/Divorce_in_the_United_States

6. No - fault divorce From Wikipedia, the free encyclopedia - en.wikipedia.org/wiki/No - fault_ divorce

7. Information on No Fault Divorce - eHow.com - C:/Documents and Settings/Owner/My Documents/... /Information on No Fault Divorce eHow.com.htm

8. NO BS Divorce Strategies for Men -http://www.greatdivorceadvice.com/index-newTestiesDLG.htm

9. No Fault Divorce History - www.divorceroom.com/no-fault-divorce/no-fault-divorce-history.html

10. History of Christian Doctrine on Divorce- divorce.lovetoknow.com/History_of_Christian_ Doctrine_on_Divorce

11. Divorce - www.spiritus-temporis.com/divorce/history of divorce.html

12. Brooks, Tim and Marsh, Earle, The Complete Directory of Prime Time Network and Cable TV shows

13. Twentieth Century-Fox episode information on The Many Loves of Dobie Gillis

14. Hickman, Dwayne, Forever Dobie: The Many Lives of Dwayne Hickman, Carol Publishing Corporation, Secaucus, New Jersey, 1994

15. The Many Loves of Dobie Gillis (http://www.tv.com/show/790/summary.html) at TV.com (http://www.imdb.com/title/tt0052490/) at the Internet Movie Database (en.

DIVORCE: WHAT AN EDUCATION

wikipedia.org/wiki/The_Many_Lives_of_Dobie_Gillis)

16. Dobie Gillis/ Classic TV (http://www.tvparty.com/recdobie.html)
17. The Affairs of Dobie Gillis (1953 film) (http://www.imdb.com/title/tt0045479) at the Internet Movie Database
18. Whatever Happen to Dobie Gillis? (1977 TV movie) (http://www.imdb.com/title/tt0486675/) at the Internet Movie Database
19. Bring Me the Head of Dobie Gillis (1988 TV movie) (http://www.imdb.com/title/tt0094800/) at the Internet Movie Database
20. Sheila Kuehl
    a. Sheila Kuehl, The Brainy Bird on Dobie Gillis, Likes to Lay Down the Law as a Professor: People:com (www.people.com/people/archieve/article/0,20092334,00.html)
    b. Sheila James Kuehl - Biography (www.imdb.com/name/nm0473861/bio)
    c. Zelda Gilroy Meltdown - Bio critics Politics (blogcritics.org/.../zelda-gilroy-meltdown)
    d. Sheila Kuehl- Wikipedia, the free encyclopedia (en.wikipedia.org/wiki/Sheila_James) www.sheila.org/home
    e. 10 Questions for Sheila Kuehl today.ucla.edu/portal/ut/10-questions- for-sheila-kuehl-208170.aspx
    f. glbtq>>social sciences>> Kuehl, Sheila James glbtq.com/social-sciences/kuehl_sj.html
    g. Issue: Child Support caltax.org/Member/...may99-5.htm

BIBLIOGRAPHY

21. Court Documentation -2003, 2004, 2005, 2006, 2007, and 2009
    1. Letter from ex-wife attorney
    2. Petition for Trial Documentation
    3. Documentation from Cydney Batchelor
        a. Deputy Trial Counsel California State Bar Association
    4. Documentation Mediation Report - Lynne Zahnley
    5. Wells Fargo Statements and Documentation
        a. 1998 Dodge Durango
    6. Disso Master Documentation
22. Child Support -Letters and Statements of payments
23. Single Parent - Wikipedia, the free encyclopedia -http://en.wikipedia.org/wiki/Single-parent
24. A Brief History of Motherhood - trueroots blog -http://www.trueroots.us/blog/2009/05/08/a-brief-history-of-motherhood/
25. Single-Parent Families - Definition, Description, Common Problems -http://www.healthofchildren.com/S/Single-Parent-Familites.html
26. Single Mothers Since 2000: Falling Farther Down
    a. Employment Characteristics of Families -http://www.bls.gov/news.release/pdf/famee.pdf.
    b. http://www.census.gov/hhes/ww/epstc/cps_table_creator.html
    c. Table F-10. Presence of Children Under 18 Years Old by Median and Mean Income: 1974-2009 -http://www.census..gove/hhes/www/income/data/historical/

families/index.html
27. Tom Leykis - Wikipedia, the free encyclopedia en.wikipedia.org/wiki/Flash_Fridays
28. Adoption - Documentation from the Court
    a. Process of Adoption
29. Personal Injury San Francisco Marysville: Horrific Speeding
    a. www.personal-injury-san-francisco.net/2012
30. Lawsuit filed in deadly Maryville crash - Appeal - Democrat.com/news/lawsuit-filed
31. Olivehurst man injured in fatal crash listed in fair condition
    a. www.appeal-democrat.com/olivehurst-man injured
32. Pedestrian who died in Marysville wreck was single mother
    a. technews.tmcnet.com/news/2012/04/12/6...
33. The Wedding Planner (2001 romantic comedy film)
    a. en.wikipedia.org/wiki/The_Wedding_Planner
34. The Patriot (2000 film)
    a. en.wikipedia.org/wiki/The_Patriot_ (2000 film)
35. Shih Tzu History - The Lion Dog (www.entirelyshihtzu.com/shih-tzu-history.html)
    a. Shih Tzu - Wikipedia, the free encyclopedia (en.wikipedia.org/wiki/Shih_Tzu)
    b. Shih Tzu, by Jaime J. Sucher, pg 5, Barron's Educational Series, 2000, ISBN 0-7641-1043-8 -Steven Allison. "Shih Tzu" (http://www.findoutaboutdogbreeds.com/Shih_Tzu.html)
    c. FindOutAboutDogBreeds.com (http://www.findoutaboutdogbreeds.com/Shih_Tzu.html) Retrieved 2007-11-07

BIBLIOGRAPHY

    d. Shih Tzu for Dummies, by Eve Adamson, pg 257, For Dummies, Publisher, 2007, ISBN 0-470-08945-8 quote: "Lady Brownrigg, who brought the first Shih Tzu into England, coined the phrase Chrysanthemum Dog"

        1. Shih Tzu for Dummies, by Eve Adamson pg 27, For Dummies, Publisher, 2007, ISBN 0-470-08945-8 e.-Shih Tzu- Wikipedia, the free encyclopedia (en.wikipedia.org/wiki/Shih_Tzu)

    e. merican Kennel Club - Shih Tzu History (www.akc.org/breeds/shih_tzu/history.cfm)

36. 8 track tape - en.wikipedia.org/wiki/8-track_tape
37. Police Report - Reno, Nevada of ex wife, Aug 2000
38. City Slickers - Wikipedia, the free encyclopedia
    a. en.wikipedia.org/wiki/City_Slickers
39. Father's Rights Movement - Wikipedia, the free encyclopedia
    a. en.wikipedia.org/wiki/Fathers%27_rights
40. Fathers' and Men's Rights Organizations, Writers and Other Leaders
    a. http://www.fathersrightsnetwork.net/groups
41. Fathers' Right Group Profile - Fathers and Families
    a. http://fatherhood.about.com//od/advocacy groups/p/Fathers-And-Families
42. Fathers' Rights Organizations - Dads America
    a. http://fatherhood.about.com/od/advocacygroups/p/Fathers-Rights-Organizations
43. Organization Profile - Dads Against Discrimination
    a. http://fatherhood.about.com/od/advocacygroups/p/Dads-Against-Discrimination

DIVORCE: WHAT AN EDUCATION

44. Fathers Rights - List of Father's Rights Groups
    a. http://fatherhood.about.com/od/advocacygroups/p/Father's-Rights-Organizations
45. Fathers Rights in California - During and After Divorce
    a. http://www.cadivorce.com/news/fathers-rights
46. Father's Rights Help - Free Fathers Rights Attorney Support and Advice
    a. http://www.familylawrights.net/fathers-rights/
47. A Promise to Ourselves - A Journey Through Fatherhood and Divorce. Alec Baldwin with Mark Tabb. Pages 205 - 211
48. The Shawshank Redemption - Wikipedia, the free encyclopedia
    a. en.wikipedia.org/wiki/The_Shawshank_ Redemption
49. Clint Black - One More Payment Lyrics - SongLyrics.com
    a. www.songlyrics.com/clint-black/one-more-payment.
50. Jaws 2 - Wikipedia, the free encyclopedia
    a. en.wikipedia.org/wiki/Jaws_2

www.ingramcontent.com/pod-product-compliance
Lightning Source LLC
Chambersburg PA
CBHW020950230426
43666CB00005B/252